IT'S EASY TO TALK JUSTICE

*A Case Study of
Hudson v Philander Smith College:
How One Woman's Case Changed My Thinking About Justice*

C . J .   D U V A L L ,   J R .

It's Easy to Talk Justice is based upon a civil rights case: *Hudson versus Philander Smith College.* Source material for the story includes: non-subpoenaed documents, a position statement submitted to the Equal Employment Opportunity Commission (EEOC) from the defendant, documents from Public Access to Court Electronic Records (PACER) database, and public information available as evidence on the Internet. Not all quotations in the book are verbatim. If not cited in the Notes section, quotations are used by the author to convey the general subject matter for readability. The author and publisher have made every effort to ensure that the information in this book is correct, and they do not assume and hereby disclaim any liability to any party for any loss, damage, or disruption caused by errors or omissions, whether such errors or omissions result from negligence, accident, or any other cause.

Palmetto Publishing Group
Charleston, SC

It's Easy to Talk Justice
Copyright © 2019 C.J. Duvall, Jr.

All rights reserved.

This book or any portion thereof may not be reproduced or used in any manner without the express written permission of the author except for use of brief quotations.

Printed in the United States of America

ISBN-13: 978-1-64111-312-0
ISBN-10: 1-64111-312-X

Dedicated to those without a voice in the room.

ONE against MANY

MANY attacked ONE
ONE stood strong

MANY would not listen
ONE carried on

MANY were silenced
ONE spoke her truth

C.J. Duvall, Jr.

Contents

Introduction
"Leadership should affirm justice, not create injustice."

vii

Chapter One
One Against Many
"There may be times when we are powerless to prevent injustice, but there must never be a time when we fail to protest."

1

Chapter Two
The Search for Truth
"We are all implicated when we allow other people to be mistreated."

16

Chapter Three
Moral Leadership
"We affirm the right of women to equal treatment in employment, responsibility, promotion, and compensation."

39

Chapter Four
Retaliation
"Man must evolve for all human conflict a method which rejects revenge, aggression and retaliation. The foundation of such a method is love."
57

Chapter Five
Dialogue
"Your silence is consent."
67

Chapter Six
Was It Worth It?
"It is easy to talk about justice. It is harder to achieve justice."
79

Epilogue
89

Notes
95

Acknowledgments
100

About the Author
102

Introduction

"Leadership should affirm justice, not create injustice."
—C.J. Duvall, Jr.

If you witnessed the violation of someone's rights would you stand up to your family, your employer, your priest, your neighbor or your friend? What would you be willing to risk standing up for justice? The answer to this question is dependent on many factors. In a personal exchange among friends discussing the risk of speaking up, loss of employment or promotional opportunity in the workplace was the most consistent theme of concern in the conversation. Following economic security, friends then cited loss of family, friends, and reputation as other compelling reasons for remaining quiet. I asked my friends, "Do we have a duty to obey the law?"

"Witnessing a violation of the law is not the same as disobeying the law. So perhaps there is no reason to speak out?" one of my friends posited.

Or is there? During this exchange, another friend replied: "Right is right. If you witness a wrong and do nothing, you may as well have done the wrong yourself. It may not always be possible or wise to directly confront the wrong-doer, but in my experience, there is always something you can do even if it is just acknowledging to the victim that a wrong has been done."

This story is about **my** decision to stand up for another person's rights, but I would argue that, as the narrative unfolds, it becomes about far more. The story covers more than three years of observations tracking an employment dispute that moved to a civil rights complaint in the case of *Hudson versus Philander Smith College*. Hudson, an alumnus and former staff member of Philander Smith College, was an ardent supporter of her alma mater and enjoyed a warm connection with the institution until her dismissal. I become involved because Hudson served in the same department that I managed at Philander Smith. It's worth noting that while I was identified as a witness, I was never subpoenaed, and neither of the parties were privy to manuscript development. The motivation to document the lawsuit was derived from conversations with cultural organizer and strategist Tufara Muhammad who cited how institutional power stifles victim complaints.

One such conversation began this way: "Institutions spread misinformation to invalidate a victim's complaint. They have various resources that overwhelm a victim. Look at any of the reported 'MeToo' incidents and you will find an impressive public persona, a well-financed legal team, and supporters inside the organization denouncing or invalidating the victim's complaint." Muhammad offered.

I couldn't talk about the details of the Hudson story so I kept the conversation focused on incidents in the public arena such as women's complaints against the Maverick's organization in Texas, Fox News, Michigan State University, and Harvey Weinstein.

I continued. "The harassment stories which have been hitting the press have brought to light the pervasiveness of harassment, which has gone on, unchecked or unaddressed, for a long time."

Muhammad countered: "But it's not just harassment. It's promotion, it's opportunity, it's retaliation, and hostile workplace environments. The root cause of much of this behavior is institutional leadership, coupled with a few close supporters in management who ignore or mask the complaints. In some cases, there are allies on the board positioned to influence other board members to believe complaints are invalid. In effect, image, money and insider support create the perfect environment to stifle the pursuit of justice for an individual. Many people in our society talk about the importance of justice but don't realize the institutional machinery at work to invalidate a victim's complaint. It doesn't have to be a sexual harassment complaint to oppress a woman."

I wrote this book to demonstrate how difficult it is to achieve justice. Nearly three years transpired from the date

Hudson experienced discrimination to the date her case ended. Her pursuit of justice took place while she sought to stabilize her economic life; care for her child; search for employment; move away for an out-of-state job (only to return again); and gather evidence for her civil case as a result of her termination from the defendant. Imagine juggling all of these responsibilities after losing a consistent paycheck. This was Hudson's challenge. Victims like Hudson have a disadvantage when fighting against institutional power because institutions can overwhelm a victim with a legitimate claim against unjust decisions. Hudson was fortunate to have retained Cox, Sterling, McClure & Vandiver, PLLC, a reputable law firm capable of challenging the power of Philander Smith College.

The story is shared in five chapters. Chapter one, titled, *One Against Many*, outlines the uphill battle Hudson faced when she challenged an institution represented by four high ranking officials in the administration, a prestigious law firm, and a board of trustees overseeing the fiduciary standing of the College. The title, *One Against Many*, portrays the circumstances under which the claimant found herself in dispute with the College. Despite lacking resources, Hudson did not give up her pursuit of justice. During this period, many of her friends and professional associates had no idea of the trials she was experiencing in trying to get her truth heard. The chapter title details the odds against Hudson being heard.

In the second chapter, *The Search for Truth*, I critique the position taken by Philander Smith College. Hudson filed an Equal Employment Opportunity Commission (EEOC) charge against Philander Smith College. Philander Smith responded to the charge in what is known as a position statement. Information in the College's statements was inconsistent with available public information, which contradicted their defense. I also describe the approach to uncover evidence supporting Hudson's position. This chapter is meant to inform both claimants and defendants of the importance of the EEOC charge response and reply process.

Chapter three dissects Philander Smith's decisions as a problem of *Moral Leadership*. Hudson was motivated to advance her case due to the College's morally questionable actions.

A description of what retaliation looked like for Hudson is outlined in chapter four, *Retaliation*. It cites events where she spoke truth to power, which were not necessarily discriminatory but were descriptive of how she sought honesty in her work relationships with the College. The ultimate betrayal of being honest while seeking a promotion ended in what she charged was a "retaliatory" act by the College.

Chapter five, titled *Dialogue*, focuses on the importance of talking through differences of opinion. Hudson wanted to discuss her differences with Philander Smith before she filed an EEOC charge, during the EEOC process and before she filed a federal law suit. It would have been less expensive and less time consuming for the College if it had agreed to an open dialogue with Hudson.

The final chapter states the implications of Hudson's story from a legal perspective and closes with a question that speaks to the matter of integrity and draws attention to the College's efforts to discredit Hudson. I invite you to study Hudson's pursuit of justice and ask, *"Was It Worth It?"*

CHAPTER ONE

One Against Many

"There may be times when we are powerless to prevent injustice, but there must never be a time when we fail to protest."
—Elie Wiesel

In the 1980s I read the work of Elie Wiesel. His work as an author exposed many people to the importance of remembering the Holocaust as a lesson to humanity to strive to fight indifference in the face of injustice. Wiesel and fellow Jews experienced monumental injustices and atrocities leading up to, and during World War II. He often spoke of the silence of others who said nothing of the brutality the victims of the Holocaust endured. His thoughts on social justice can be applied to the rights of individuals suffering injustice due to the silence of individuals in positions of moral authority. He wrote, "*There* may be times when *we* are powerless to prevent *injustice, but* there must never be a time when we fail to protest." Similarly, this book is a protest against the unjust method by which Philander Smith College crafted a story to justify the termination of Hudson, the plaintiff.

Somewhere around February 22, 2016, Gemessia Hudson was terminated from her alma mater, Philander Smith College, where she had served as a development officer in the Office of Institutional Advancement. Hudson had been employed with the College for more than three-and-a- half years. During the course of her employment she reported to a male vice president who was later replaced by a male director. Later, she reported to another male director and finally worked for me when I became Vice-President of Institutional Advancement. After I left, Hudson worked for another male director. Cumulatively, during Hudson's employment, she reported directly to four males.

The last male she reported to was a former classmate of hers from her time in college. He had returned to work at the College after a stint at the United Negro College Fund (UNCF) in Washington, D.C. where he had served as a relationship manager, facilitating workshops to encourage young people to apply for scholarships with the Gates Millennium Scholars program in partnership with the UNCF. Hudson was not enthusiastic about her former classmate being selected as her new boss because she had already asked to be considered for promotion twice, to the role he occupied. Her reaction was reasonable, she had raised several hundreds of thousands of dollars in the last two years and the new incumbent had no relevant experience in institutional fundraising.

Shortly after the new director took on his role, he was questioned about his understanding of cultivating new donors. He was not familiar with cultivation or what it entailed. Hudson and another employee were surprised the new director was not familiar with cultivation. This revelation produced concern for Hudson.

She told me, "If he doesn't know what cultivation of donors is, what else doesn't he know?" About twenty days after his hire she called me to vent.

"He is hounding me about every minute of my day, asking me to share my calendar with him so he can track where I am," she said.

Hudson and I had a good working relationship, so she frequently bounced ideas around with me or asked me for advice.

I explained to her, "Managers have the right to monitor your schedule so don't push back. He doesn't understand how fundraising works so help him get adjusted by cooperating."

It wasn't too long before Hudson called to say, "He doesn't want to share my calendar anymore."

"What prompted the change of heart?" I asked.

"I had been accused of having a meeting without him. I told him he should have used the calendar he requested. It plainly shows my meeting obligations."

It sounded like her director was using the tool to simply keep up with her activity rather than using it to coordinate meetings and facilitate productivity.

"I think he is just trying to figure out what the heck fundraising is! He doesn't seem to know much about how a development office works," I said.

Whatever his intentions, his request backfired on him when he discovered her calendar was full of meetings and call activities. It sounded as if Hudson may have been concerned, he was overwhelmed with the new commitment.

Hudson was a very productive fundraiser. She used her time efficiently, operating on a flex-time schedule so she could drop her daughter off at day care before reporting to work each morning. I didn't mind. She was bringing in a lot of money. I didn't foresee any problems for her until I received a call from her. She called me from Texas while she was with her mother. She had taken Family Medical Leave (FML) but her management team was calling her to do work while she was out.

"Should my management team be asking me to work while I am on leave?" she asked.

"Call Human Resources and ask what the proper process is and then follow it. Employers are not allowed to give assignments to you while you are on job protected leave. Ask the HR director to notify the management team of the rule and get it in writing."

Despite the fact the College was put on notice, Hudson was summoned to travel out of state to work on a UNCF-sponsored event over a weekend. She returned late Sunday evening, February 21, 2016. Upon returning to work in her Little Rock office the following day Hudson was terminated for tardiness by the director who was hired about 35 working days earlier. Hudson was shocked. She called several people close to her before calling me with the news. She didn't understand why her successful performance in the fundraising role did not protect her from a seemingly small infraction, especially since the entire office used flex-time and she had not been written up by the new director. She decided to ask me if I knew an attorney.

"I know several attorneys. Austin Porter, Jr., is a good attorney. He has represented my godson. I trust him explicitly. I don't know John Coulter personally but you might want to call him. Melanie McClure Mitchell is someone I know very well. She is a partner at Cox, Sterling, McClure & Vandiver, PLLC."

Hudson did not sit idle after her termination. She had a toddler to feed so she was putting resumes in wherever she could. She also called Philander Smith College to ask for reconsideration to return. I thought it was a good idea. I thought perhaps the new director may have acted brashly due to his inexperience and the College would recognize they just lost a great fundraiser and re-instate her. I was wrong. Apparently, her appeal to return to her old job didn't go well. Hudson was informed she would not be brought back to her alma mater. She challenged the appeal by saying she was capable of serving as a director. In answer, the College sent her a letter indicating she did not have the qualifications to serve as a director. At first, Hudson was devastated. Then she became incensed.

"Are you kidding me?! I have seven years of fundraising experience. Kevin doesn't have the same type of experience."

She was referring to her male director of 35 working days.

Shock for Hudson did not end with the denial of her appeal. The College challenged her unemployment compensation request. Usually, employers will not challenge an unemployment compensation request unless the terminated employee has broken a work rule or quit. She had not broken a work rule, nor did she quit her job. But during the unemployment hearing the College produced a document she had never seen before. The document was a disciplinary form which included new, additional reasons for termination, inferring she broke a work place rule. According to Hudson, her director presented it in the unemployment compensation hearing as 'proof' of her failure to follow rules on the job.

"I had never seen the form before. There was no date on it. There was no signature on the form," she noted.

A signature of any kind would have indicated she was present during the disciplinary session which would have also included Human Resources. What was disturbing about the College's story was that, on almost every occasion of a disciplinary action, the Human Resource director would have been present for such a meeting and would have written a note on the form indicating the date of said occasion. If there was a refusal to sign, the representative would have documented this in the presence of the employee. None of this protocol was provided in the paperwork used to seal her fate. She was denied unemployment benefits for breaking a rule. There would be no safety net for her or her daughter. At this point, Hudson was infuriated and, rightfully so. First, she knew she was passed over for a position by a male who had less experience. Second, she was terminated while she still had two days left before her finalized Family Medical Leave Act (FMLA) paperwork was due, therefore, the college violated the FMLA. Third, she was denied an appeal to return to her job. Last, and most outrageously, she was denied unemployment benefits for a reason the college would not be able to defend. In my thirty years of employment management I had never seen a more callous act of indifference shown toward another person.

Not long after being rejected for unemployment benefits in the Spring of 2016, Hudson filed an Equal Employment Opportunity Commission (EEOC) charge. The EEOC is responsible for enforcing federal laws which make it illegal to discriminate against an employee based on their race, color, religion, sex, national origin, age, disability or genetic information. Hudson's charge was one of 91,503 charges filed against U.S. employers in 2016. Her charge alleged promotion discrimination and retaliation based on gender, as well as a violation of the FMLA. Her submission of the charge was on advice of her attorney. It would be nearly seven months later before she would hear about her case status from the EEOC.

In late November of 2016, Hudson called me with a worried tone in her voice. After several months of silence, she still had not heard back from the EEOC investigator.

"I know you have experience in this area, and I don't want to call my attorney every time I have a question. What should I do?" she asked.

The experience she was referring to was my previous career investigating Equal Employment Opportunity Commission (EEOC) charges. I suggested she call the EEOC office and ask for an update on her charge file. I did not expect to hear back from her so quickly but within a day or two, she called me with a bomb shell. Sobbing, she described a document given to her by the EEOC.

"I can't believe this, you have to read this."

I was exhausted from a day of work, it was late evening. I needed to retire for the night so I suggested we meet the following day.

As planned, I drove to her new workplace to review the document. Over her lunch break, we reviewed everything together. The document, called a 'position statement' contained Philander Smith College's response to her charge of discrimination. In it was the employer's response to the alleged charge of discrimination filed by Hudson. Typically, the statement is drafted by an attorney or Human Resources person after interviewing the management members involved in the employment decision causing the charge of discrimination. The interviewer then transcribes their comments into an official position on what happened, otherwise known as a position statement. Under a policy implemented on January 1, 2016, the EEOC permits claimants like Hudson to request a copy of the position statement to see what the employer said about them. The document was not secret so Hudson asked me to read the eight-page response to Hudson's charges of discrimination. Philander Smith College alleged Hudson violated a signature signing policy; did not apply for, or express interest in a promotion to director; had no experience in national fundraising; and had a record of misconduct. Furthermore, the College stated the male director that was hired over Hudson was the most qualified individual for the position and had relevant national fundraising experience. Hudson was upset with the characterization, saying, "It is not true."

The College had the resources to spend money on the Chambers USA number 1 ranked law firm in Arkansas to write the statement. The law firm conducted staff interviews to collect information against her charge of discrimination. Ultimately, the position statement was written by an attorney of the prestigious firm retained for the college. The law firm had an excellent reputation in employment law; in fact, I used the firm for immigration work when I served in the international division of Alltel Information Services, Inc. (formerly Systematics, Inc.). The firm even worked with some of my mentees from Philander Smith College. I admired them for their work. I still do today. But my admiration did not cloud what I read. There, in black and white was a story I *knew* had several misrepresentations of Hudson. She could tell I was shocked, and she nodded silently, feeling affirmed in her emotions. I read the position statement over and over in disbelief, until I began to weep. Up until this time, nearly eight months after her termination, I had not understood what she had endured. I was somewhat out of the picture with regard to her complaint – at least up until I read the position statement submitted by the College. I asked myself, "How could members of management representing the moral leadership of a social justice school provide misleading statements so easily contradicted by simple online investigation? How could the position statement refer to Hudson's work history and exclude more than two years of outstanding documented performance? Why did the college terminate Hudson for something other male employees historically did without disciplinary action? And furthermore, could easily be disputed with requested discovery? Where was the truth?"

I was saddened that the position statement, though skillfully written, had missing information in some portions and was filled with mis-characterizations of Hudson. The document was absent of any mention of her success in raising significant amounts of funds for the college. She had raised more money than the two previous male directors of development combined. The absence of the mention of her superior performance was painful when listening to her describe her situation. This was a strange decision to terminate the best fundraiser in the office when it would not have cost the college a dime to reconsider their decision.

After reading the College's position statement, I began to question the school's ethics. How does an institution of social justice, promoting timeless human values, fail to honor the truth? I was ashamed to have publicly supported an administration that claimed higher ground in the public arena, but privately helped author a document that could destroy a person with innuendo. I am certain the school didn't know the position statement could be shared with Hudson; otherwise why would they have composed a response with information that was not true and could be challenged legally? Or, perhaps they were expecting a challenge. Executive board members usually make the decision to engage a law firm. Non-executive trustees are generally unaware of the details. They are usually dependent on the judgement of the president and the executive committee to evaluate risks. Instead of mediating with Hudson in May of 2016, the College elected to fight Hudson. She was going to face at least four obstacles.

Four Obstacles

The first obstacle Hudson would face would be the legal cost of challenging the College when they elected to defend her challenge. Legal challenges are expensive, reaching into the hundreds of millions of dollars annually for hundreds of employment lawsuits across the United States. Over the course of my professional life I have observed, investigated, mediated, or testified across a range of employment disputes. Litigation is a long, burdensome and expensive struggle for justice. While our system of justice is not perfect, our system is necessary; in matters under the law, two parties can face off in the court system. It is a pity many complaints are not resolved without going to court. In my experience, many complaints can be resolved with dialogue. The simple act of talking through disagreements can circumvent long tortuous periods of litigation draining time, mental energy, and financial resources that are better used elsewhere. The College could have engaged in conversation with Hudson rather than terminating one of its most productive employees.

The second obstacle for Hudson would be the task of taking on four, high-level representatives of the College: a charismatic president, a talented vice-president, and two directors. All of them were connected in some way, to the content of the position statement if by nothing more than to have provided information to the attorney, or to have read and approved the final position statement. Attorneys generally do not create a position statement without the aid of the defendant. They need thoughtful client feedback to produce multiple-page responses. In my opinion, the way in which the position statement was crafted, may have been meant to destroy Hudson's credibility in the eyes of the EEOC. It was convincing both in tone and in legal nomenclature.

A third obstacle Hudson would contend with was the College's law firm, Cross, Gunter, Witherspoon & Galchus, P.C. (CGWG). Very few people can match the fire power of a big law firm like CGWG. It was unlikely Hudson could have prevailed without help from a talented law firm that could go toe-to-toe with the lawyers representing Philander Smith College.

A fourth, indirect but influential obstacle Hudson would face would be the board of trustees who were charged with supporting the president and the institution in the forward progress of the College. Having been a trustee of the same institution, I know it was rare for a trustee to truly understand the details of what happens in day-to-day ground-level operations. Trustees rely on college administration to inform them of related business. It isn't unusual or unreasonable for a board to stand with the school's administration. Why wouldn't they? It's their charge and responsibility to support the leadership. Besides, why would close to twenty people, with successful resumes and backgrounds stand up for Hudson, who was an alleged "rule breaker," reported by leadership as having a "poor attendance record?" Some members would think Hudson deserved to have been fired. The information presented to them by college leadership would justify termination. In defense of the trustees, they had no real optics into the truth of the allegations in the case. They didn't have all of the facts. Unfortunately for Hudson, there would be no moral "voice in the room" to speak on her behalf. The story was rigged in my opinion. Indirectly, the board authorized the use of legal counsel; supported the administration that made the decision; and failed to create a path to dialogue before terminating Hudson.

At this stage, the cost to challenge the management team, face a prestigious law firm and a notable board of trustees, represented the monumental obstacles that stood in the way of Hudson's pursuit of justice. Despite the powerful contingent of people positioned to fight against her, Hudson decided to challenge Philander Smith College; the school of civil rights leaders; the school of a former U.S. Surgeon General Jocelyn Elders; the school of renowned theologian James Cone, and many famous physicians, teachers, scientists, preachers and business leaders. She was challenging the College knowing she had to face the management team who made the decision to endanger the economic security of her family. She realized her alma mater would use their finances to form a defense against her, even though many of the stakeholders did not know the real story. She was broken hearted. She wanted to tell her story to someone but no one was there to hear it, or heal it in the tradition of a compassionate community of reconciliation. She never would have fought her alma mater if there had been an advocate in the room to support her position. There was only an EEOC position statement with a set of false statements concerning matters of injustice. Elie Wiesel once said, concerning matters of injustice, "We must take sides. Neutrality helps the oppressor, never the victim. Silence encourages the tormentor, never the tormented. Sometimes we must interfere."

Hudson was aware of the obstacles she faced and she knew it would be difficult to fight the College. She expected to be maligned for standing up for herself. When she decided to fight-back she was one against many. I decided not to be neutral.

CHAPTER TWO

The Search for Truth

"We are all implicated when we allow other people to be mistreated."
—Bryan Stevenson, *Just Mercy*

In a January 18, 2017 press release, the U.S. Equal Employment Opportunity Commission reported 26,934 sex discrimination charges and 42,018 retaliation charges were filed in 2016 the previous year. Hudson's charges were included in these numbers as well as discrimination related to a disability violation. More than 90.6 percent of EEOC cases achieved a successful resolution. When I read the Philander Smith College position statement I realized her charge would not be resolved at the EEOC level. The employer was not intent on resolving her charge in the Spring of 2016 when it occurred. Hudson's charge would escalate to a federal civil rights case. According to the written position statement, the charge was: (1) "Discrimination because of association with an individual alleged to have a disability in violation of the Americans with

Disabilities Act of 1991 (ADA); (2) Discrimination on the basis of her sex because she was allegedly denied a promotion in violation of Title VII of the Civil Rights Act of 1964 (Title VII); and (3) Retaliation because she allegedly made a complaint of discrimination in violation of Title VII." [Philander Smith College Position Statement, May 2, 2016, page 2-3]. The College denied discriminating against Ms. Hudson.

Hudson told the EEOC investigator the entire defense by the College was not accurate. I think to be blunt, she said, "It is not true." The EEOC explained to her she needed to send a reply back to the EEOC by December 8, 2016. It was the last week of November. She didn't have much time. I explained to Hudson she needed to break the position statement down into parts to reply to the misrepresentations. It was easier said than done.

"I don't know how to respond to the EEOC. Is there a format?" she asked.

"Go to the EEOC website to see if there is a FAQ link providing guidance to claimants or ask your EEOC investigative contact. The most important aspect is to find information you can use in your response to show why your claim is valid, and why their response is invalid. You just can't call the College's position untrue: You will have to provide evidence to support your position.

Hudson was stymied by the pressure of drafting a response. She created a draft of notes but the notes did not represent a response. It was in the midst of the holiday season, between Thanksgiving and Christmas. She didn't have the money to pay her lawyer in the endeavor to write a response to the EEOC. She needed to save her finances for a lawsuit. It was Hudson and not her attorney who interviewed me about my understanding of her employment tenure.

"It would be easier if you gave me a list of questions to answer. I will write my responses to your questions so you can include them in your response."

I was speaking from the position of someone familiar with the EEOC process. Conversely, she was utterly unfamiliar with anything related to the charge process. I collaborated with her on writing the draft so she could meet her already stated earlier deadline.

I told her, "I cannot stand by and watch the College write false things about you. It could destroy your career."

We worked over the phone, reading sections of the document aloud to discuss the contents of the position statement. Hudson had read the document several times. Each time we reviewed it, she would react with anger and hurt reliving the events and emotions all over again. One of the sections of the position statement referring to her former director and boss read:

> "…he engaged in significant development, recruiting, and fundraising activities. He was selected for the position via Presidential Proclamation in November 2015." [Philander

Smith College Position Statement, Charging Party: Gemessia Hudson Charge No. 493-2016-00958, May 2, 2016, page 3].

Hudson shrieked, "This statement is not true! I have seven years of fundraising experience. He does not. How can they say he engaged in significant fundraising activities?"

I had known Hudson's new director since his college days when he ate chicken enchiladas, beans and rice at my house in 2006. I knew his career arc from seminary, to working as an admissions counselor, to working as a program facilitator scheduling workshops for the UNCF.

"I know he doesn't have significant fundraising experience. You will be able to refute their story." I reassured.

"How can I refute their story?" Hudson asked.

"With public information anyone can find." I replied.

While Hudson and I were on the phone I used my desktop search engine to track her directors' work activities. The internet provided a lot of information. I shared the following with Hudson:

"In October of 2013, he facilitated the UNCF 'Empower Me' tour. The Empower Me Tour was not fundraising. It was an information tour promoting the Gates Millennium Scholars college scholarship. He was a workshop organizer."

I continued, "In June of 2014, he is shown listed as 'Relationship Manager' with the Gates Millennium Scholars Program facilitating a workshop in Jacksonville, Florida. In

December 2014, it appears he facilitated another scholarship workshop in Dallas, Texas, the same month he met with me in Washington D.C. for a meeting with his management team."

"Wait a minute," Hudson interjected. You met with him in Washington D.C., at the UNCF?"

"Yes, I went to UNCF headquarters in D.C. The day after I visited with the UNCF, I went to see Ron Newsome, Harry Roberson and Sterling King on Saturday. I went to church on Sunday with Harry Roberson and Ron Newsome."

Hudson was silent, probably incredulous regarding my visit to UNCF headquarters. It turned out to be serendipitous. I visited UNCF headquarters to see her future director and boss a year before he was hired by the College. I returned to reading the Internet evidence. I read aloud: "Philander Smith College hosted an informational scholarship workshop on April 15, 2015, during which your boss was the presenter. On Friday, September 18, 2015, at Dillard University he is listed as the contact for the scholarship program."

"All of this is on the internet?"

"I kid you not. The very month you were informed he was hired over you to direct fundraising, an announcement lists him as the key contact for a bridge builders scholarship meeting at UCLA on Sunday, November 15, 2015."

Hudson said, "Wow. None of the time was spent fundraising like the College insinuates. The College doesn't know this information is on the Internet?"

"No. They probably don't know there is evidence contradicting their defense. Everything I shared is searchable and public. Their attorney certainly didn't know any better. If he had done a public search on his client, he never would have crafted a story about his client engaging in "significant fundraising" activity while said client was actually "scheduling workshops" with students. But that's not all I have." I said to Hudson.

"I searched my travel calendar to be sure my UNCF meeting with him was documented. I found my trip records with expense notes confirming I visited the UNCF in Washington, D.C. During the trip I met his supervisor, Ms. Kimberly Hall, Director of Program Services, Ms. Paulette Jackson, Vice-President of Development and Mr. Maurice E. Jenkins, Jr., Executive Vice President of National Development. I kept a record of the meeting."

"Okay," replied Hudson, "and...."

"Well, in this same meeting Ms. Hall explained the Gates Millennium Scholars program was designed to encourage students to apply for UNCF scholarships. She and Ms. Paulette Jackson explained that, fundraising was managed through regional development offices staffed around the country. You should ask your lawyer to seek an affidavit from Hall or Jackson to verify he did not engage in daily fundraising. With this information your attorney can depose the College selection committee as to how on earth he, with no demonstrable fundraising experience, was selected to be the next director of development for an office that had a two and one half million-dollar annual office goal, yet he had no demonstrable fundraising experience?"

This was important evidence that was easily discoverable. I wondered why the president, or the director of human resources of the school was defending the selection of the new director as being a superior selection decision to Hudson's candidacy when available public information was inconsistent with their written defense? I wondered how any of the management team's commitment to fairness factored into supporting the position of the College. I was disappointed. These were my friends and colleagues attacking Hudson.

Gathering job information on her former director became easier as Hudson and I brainstormed sources. She called a contact at the UNCF to ask if the male director was a fundraiser while working there. Her contact responded, "Who?" According to Hudson, the UNCF contact was a senior level development person who knew all of the regional development officers within the UNCF. Her contact stated solidly, "He was not a fundraiser." Hudson's contact also corroborated the information from Paulette Jackson, vice president of development at the UNCF.

At this stage in our search, we were able to gather evidence to indicate Hudson's former director was a former relationship program manager with the UNCF, with no daily fundraising background or responsibility. Our next question was, "Who selected him to oversee the fundraising arm of the College with no demonstrable knowledge or experience?" The College states:

> "…He was selected for the position via Presidential Proclamation in November 2015." [Philander Smith College Position Statement, Charging Party: Gemessia Hudson, Charge No. 493-2016-00958, May 2, 2016, page 3].

Selection decisions are often governed by a set of legal guidelines to protect applicants from discrimination which is why processes for selection are often challenged if they exclude a qualified candidate from being able to compete. Companies or institutions like Philander Smith College that receive federal funding, must be very careful not to violate the Civil Rights Act of 1967 (as amended). The college states they "do not tolerate discrimination or harassment, or retaliation for engaging in any protected conduct." Yet, the college selected an inexperienced male candidate whose public credentials supported Hudson's allegation that she was a victim of discrimination. Her former director's selection was discriminatory. Who selected him? The position statement does not state the name of the person who selected the male candidate. The document simply states he was selected via "Presidential Proclamation." I have read a great deal about selection procedures governed by equal employment opportunity; I have never come across an instance where Presidential Proclamation is protected against a discrimination lawsuit.

Hudson chided me, "C'mon, you know who selected him. You didn't select him. The human resources director didn't select him. The president selected him! What do you think Presidential Proclamation means? The president notified me, Rosalyn and Yvonne on November 17, 2015, another male director was joining us in December of 2015."

Rosalyn and Yvonne worked in the office with Hudson. Rosalyn was a development coordinator, and Yvonne was the head of Alumni Affairs. Both of them would have to be called as witnesses to testify about the selection decision.

Hudson continued, "The position was never posted internally or externally. I was excluded from consideration and the College will have to explain why they didn't post the job."

"I agree, but you should anticipate the College might manufacture another story when you get to trial."

Despite the public evidence indicating the new male director had no relevant experience, the College pursued their line of thinking in the document by stating the new director had national fundraising experience and Hudson had no experience on national fundraising campaigns. I knew better. Here is what the College wrote:

> "Mr. Cooper's relevant experience in national fundraising outweighed Charging Party's experience," and [Charging Party] "had no

experience on national fundraising campaigns." [Philander Smith College Position Statement, Charging Party: Gemessia Hudson, Charge No. 493-2016-00958, May 2, 2016, page 3].

This statement was patently false when one considered the new director's publicly advertised workshop facilitator activity for the UNCF. His actual record undercut the assertion of "relevant experience in national fundraising," especially when one took into account Hudson's very real previous experience in 2014, at which time she replaced a male director to serve as the campaign liaison to the national Last Mile Campaign sponsored by the National Alumni Association, Philander Smith College, Inc., (NAAPSC). The Last Mile campaign was a national fundraiser for Philander Smith College supporting the College's capital campaign. Ms. Hudson was a development officer entrusted with serving as the liaison in place of a director who was dismissed from the project at the request of the NAAPSC Last Mile committee. How do I know Hudson replaced the dismissed male director to serve as liaison to a national fundraising campaign? Because I was present at the time the decision was made, and I was the vice president who made the decision. The Last Mile campaign reached over 20 chapters and hundreds of alumni living around the country, including California, New York, Missouri, Oklahoma, Illinois, Indiana, Ohio, Michigan, Maryland, Virginia, Mississippi,

Texas, Louisiana, Tennessee, Arkansas, and even the District of Columbia. Hudson's experience was truly national in terms of fundraising assignments, outreach, and development. The new director had none of this experience when the college mounted a defense against Ms. Hudson's charge of discrimination.

"All of the work I have put into being a development officer is being attacked. What is written in their position statement is not true," she would vent.

By now, in reading and analyzing the story presented by the College, I recognized the accusations made by the school about Ms. Hudson's alleged lack of experience and poor work performance could likely be viewed dimly by the EEOC, or by a court if she were to press forward with a civil complaint by herself. She wanted to fight to set the record straight. I warned her if she thought reading the position statement was nasty, she was in for a rude awakening if she was granted a "right to sue" letter by the EEOC.

"It will get tougher, before any resolution is reached and the College will likely create more misrepresentations. No one in authority on the board knows your true story. No one in the general public knows your true story. The College's attorneys may not actually know your story. Their job is to formulate a defense despite the bad information the College created. It is going to get real ugly because you will be looked upon as the pariah."

"I know it is going to get worse but someone needs to know the true story."

I thought to myself, "How many people have experienced this moment?" Hudson's professional reputation was being rewritten by the College not just by a report to the board, but in a civil challenge. It would leave her with emotional scars. She would forever remember her management team at Philander Smith College denied her appeal to return to work and denied her unemployment benefits based upon false information.

Just to underscore the seriousness of her battle ahead, I repeated my warning. "The denial of your appeal, and the denial of your unemployment based upon the information supplied by the College is an omen of the brutality of a trial. The College is seeking to quash your story, dismiss your charge, or fight your future civil rights complaint. In my opinion, some of the material they are using is false. You must prove the College broke the law."

Hudson responded, "I must fight this so it does not happen to another woman again. They know what they did, and it was wrong."

The next day Hudson went back to work. We scheduled another phone call for after business hours. I have to admit I was tired. My schedule was hectic. Her schedule was even more so with work and a toddler she had to look after.

I continued studying the "facts" presented by the College. The next statement was concerning Ms. Hudson's alleged "history of misconduct." [Philander Smith College Position Statement, Charging Party: Gemessia Hudson, Charge No. 493-2016-00958, May 2, 2016, page 4].

The history of misconduct the college alleged to have occurred took place in 2013, when Ms. Hudson reported to an inexperienced fundraising director that replaced the previous vice president before my hire. He wrote Ms. Hudson up for "unacceptable attendance." I was on campus during this period, teaching a class in the business school and serving as a co-chair on the capital campaign. I was present during this period, frequenting the Office of Institutional Advancement to work on campaign details. I observed firsthand the difference between the two male directors' latitude to come and go during the work day without governance. Neither was disciplined or written up. The women in their office made jokes about deliberately parking their cars in different spots. Their male supervisor would fret about their attendance or if they were on time if he didn't see their cars parked in proximity of the building. Time and attendance seemed to be the central focus of the fundraising director's work. He missed the fact that development officers needed to meet with prospects, cultivate new donors, and visit with existing donors off campus, before, during and after work. His key focus should have been productive fundraising. If the focus was on attendance without understanding the work, then disciplinary write-ups labeled as misconduct should have been the norm for any fundraiser in the office regardless of gender.

During this same period, an experienced senior-level female professional capable of running the Office of Institutional Advancement left Philander Smith College to take a director job with another institution. A few years later, I asked her about her departure. She replied, "I didn't see any opportunity for me, especially when the director I reported to had no development credentials." Philander Smith College had already passed over a qualified female previous to Hudson's complaint and Hudson knew it.

Our evening call covered the College's language about Hudson's misconduct in 2013, once again setting off a roller-coaster of emotion.

"Can you believe they are using a write up created by a man with no development or fundraising management experience characterizing me as having misconduct?" Hudson vented.

"Their strategy is to use any information they can to tarnish you. Ignore the misinformation from 2013. You know it is false. Your complaint is not about what happened in 2013. Stay focused on 2014-2016. The information they are using won't be helpful to the College's defense. Their attempt at misinformation may give the College leadership a sense of security, but your confidence will have to come from presenting the irrefutable truth. If you stick with the 'truth,' it won't matter."

"How do I reply to the EEOC?" asked Hudson.

"You tell the truth through comparison. Let them know you are prepared to compare and depose all three male directors you have worked with between 2014-2016. I read through the College's statement and have created a chart to compare you with each of the males. I know all of them and I know the entire office. You might as well give your side of the case now to the others so they can see you are prepared to dismantle their defense by using their own male selection decisions as evidence of bias."

"I don't understand." said Hudson.

"The chart I created compares everyone's fundraising success, past work experience, and performance evaluations. Your response to the EEOC should include these comparisons in writing. It will counter the position statement submitted by the College and create reasonable doubt in the mind of the EEOC."

"How will that help me?" queried Hudson.

"The comparison will illustrate your success and depth in fundraising. It could help you win the support of the EEOC if they see your alternative narrative. It's possible they could decide to take on your case to challenge the College." I reasoned.

"Do you mean the EEOC will take the College to court on my behalf?" asked Hudson.

'Yes," I answered, "but if it doesn't win their support, they will give you a right to sue the College."

I believed the chart comparison would be critical information to use in her court case. Hudson's attorney could use it to ask each male about their work history and respective performances. The College's witnesses would embarrass them in court.

"May I have a copy of the chart?" asked Hudson.

"Sure. Much of the information is based upon the knowledge I acquired while working at the College, a fact the College intentionally omitted in the position statement for good reason. They didn't want the EEOC to know there was a different story, which explains why the College hid the entire period of your employment from their attorney. They definitely concealed it from the EEOC."

My understanding of Hudson's skill and success came about when I became the vice president of the Office of Institutional Advancement in June 2014. My assignment in the department allowed me to oversee fundraising activity of the staff. During the time Hudson reported to me she asked me for a promotion. I told her I believed she was ready for a manager position, and quite possibly a director-level position in twelve to eighteen months. I appreciated Hudson's competitiveness. She worked hard raising money while presenting the College in a professional light and engendering good favor among her donors. Donors loved Hudson. I never had a performance problem with her; in fact, she was so ambitious about her career she asked me how she could become a director soon after a colleague announced he was leaving the position for another job. I recall telling her, "If you can handle director-level work successfully by completing the director-level assignments, I will recommend you for promotion again."

The assignments were: (1) Serve as the chairperson of the first ever Scholarship Gala; (2) Drive the creation of a new scholarship fund entitled the '1877 to Infinity Scholarship

Fund'; and (3) Raise $25,000 at the 2015 Fall Homecoming. I was so impressed with her ambition I offered her the same type of commitment to her fundraising efforts I had offered to a male director in fundraising. I told Hudson I would match the $25,000 if she secured the first $25,000. All of these tasks were big assignments because they all coincided concurrently. As chair of the Gala, she oversaw a committee of seven people, something a director should easily be able to accomplish. As the sole 1877 to Infinity Scholarship development officer, she created the fundraising plan and set off to be successful on the Homecoming campaign. The Monday after the Homecoming weekend, she came to my office with the fundraising accounting report reconciled against cash and check acceptances. She had more than $32,000.

"Next year you should ask for a dollar-for-dollar match."

We laughed, celebrating the success she brought with her efforts. I knew she was ready for a director position and by then, the position she sought was vacant.

The position statement submitted by the College had absolutely no information about her success; no mention of her exceptional performance evaluation; no mention of my requests to the president to promote her, and no consideration for the position that did not get posted during my employment, which ended a week after the new director showed up. Instead, the College resurrected a litany of false information about her past. The position statement read:

> "the Charging Party's behavior and attitude with her supervisors did not resolve…" [Philander Smith College Position Statement, Charging Party: Gemessia Hudson, Charge No. 493-2016-00958, May 2, 2016, page 4].

Chronologically, the statement, "Hudson's behavior with her supervisors did not resolve," was false. Hudson's behavior and her attitude were stellar from 2014 to 2015. She was the best fundraiser in the office, outperforming her male counterparts. The statement made by the College was simply not true.

"How do we disprove all of this?" Hudson asked. "None of it is true but…"

I cut her off and responded, "The evidence is mostly public evidence with some of the more private information stored on the College's fundraising database. There is other evidence too. Do you have copies of the brochures for the programs you created?"

"Yes." said Hudson.

"Good. Use it to create an inventory. You developed the new Minton Legacy Society campaign and presented the concept to the National Alumni Association at the convention. Get copies of the brochures you created and call the alumni who signed up for the Minton Legacy Society. You will need them when you go to trial. The College won't give you the planned gift information. They will likely hide it. But that will be disclosed at trial so don't fret. You will need a copy of the brochure for the '1877 to Infinity Scholarship campaign'. I still have a tri-fold if you need one."

Hudson excitedly offered up, "What about the first annual President's Scholarship Gala? I was the chair for the program."

"Yes. Did you keep a copy of the program? It has your name listed as the chairperson in charge of the Gala's fundraising, along with all of the staff who worked with you. If you have anything you produced, created, led, or authored, find it. We will demonstrate you outperformed your male counterparts by the sheer amount of work materials available to the public."

Hudson also offered, "I have 'congratulations' and 'thank you' notes commending me on my work from alumni, including Ron Newsome, Sherman Tate, and Lou Ethel Nauden. I also have a note from Carmelita Smith thanking me for working on her mother's endowment balance. I have my notes from Mrs. Nauden's endowment questions as well."

"Save whatever you have. You may need it when we get to trial."

While we gathered more evidence of Hudson's successes I continued helping her write the remaining part of the draft reply. Hudson submitted screenshots and copies of FMLA related correspondence from the College which, frankly, was beyond my scope of expertise. I told her to retain the information for her attorney because I thought it might prove the College retaliated against her by terminating her under job protected leave. Her attorney would have to address this charge.

We had almost completed writing her reply when Hudson asked about the College's statement charging her with violating a college signature policy on a 'Memorandum of Understanding.'

"How can the College say I violated a signature policy when there was not a written policy particular to 'Memorandums of Understanding'?" she asked.

"I don't know." I responded. "They can say anything they want in their current position."

I was sensitive to her question. I signed 'Memorandums of Understanding' frequently without such a policy in place. If the memorandum is considered to be a contract, then I violated the policy as well. The president would sign the same document after me days later. I never got in trouble. Terminating Hudson for the same thing I did was a double standard. The most disconcerting aspect of the College's position statement is that it called attention to an area of inappropriate stewardship I reported to the president while I was still employed with the College.

"I have something to tell you. All of this time I have been asking you to look for evidence of public information on the Internet or in your personal files. I never realized until this moment, when you asked about 'Memorandums of Understanding,' that there is another source of evidence to substantiate your position."

"What is it?" she asked.

"Personal correspondence to me from the president. The letter he gave me is not consistent with the position statement explanation for your termination. The letter states the College does not have a clear set of fundraising policies. It's dated April 13, 2016, nearly two months after your termination."

"That's great C.J.!"

Her excitement was warranted. Having a document signed by the College's president would be a powerful piece of evidence she could use to vindicate herself from the gross misrepresentation in the position statement.

I was happy for her but I was not excited about the prospect of releasing my letter from the president of the College to the EEOC, or to anyone else. The letter was connected to a much broader topic of concern than a simple policy on signing 'Memorandums of Understanding' for endowments. While the letter would support Hudson if used in a public trial, I was certain the testimony could bleed into another area I had hoped the College would address privately for their own sake. Personally, I hoped no one would subpoena the letter but if it meant vindicating Hudson then the truth had to be shared.

I completed writing the reply to the EEOC by December 8, 2016. I penned it in third person, clearly indicating Hudson was no longer "one against many." The opposing counsel would know she had help writing it. In the words of social justice activist and founder of the Equal Justice Initiative, Bryan Stevenson, "We are all implicated when we allow other people to be mistreated." It was appropriate for me to help. I did not think the president, the human resources director, or anyone from the College would be able to withstand the withering questions of Hudson's attorney after discovery was complete. By December 8, 2016, these were the facts:

1. The College submitted an error-filled position statement to the EEOC.

2. The new director was a former recruiter and later a workshop facilitator with a title of 'Relationship Manager.'

3. The new director had no relevant fundraising experience at a national level.

4. Hudson had worked on a national fundraising campaign and the male director had not.

5. The male director was selected by 'Presidential Proclamation.'

6. The new inexperienced male director terminated Hudson only 35 business days after he began work.

7. The fundraising chart showed Hudson raised more money in two years than three male directors combined in the same period.

8. The College lost thousands of dollars when they hired the new male director and terminated Hudson.

9. No one from the social justice department of the College stepped forward to share the truth in defense of Hudson.

By December of 2016, the story was as much about the person as it was the principle. Things had become predictably and unavoidably personal.

—⚌—

CHAPTER THREE

Moral Leadership

"We affirm the right of women to equal treatment in employment, responsibility, promotion, and compensation."
—[Social Principles of the United Methodist Church]

The spark that flames a dispute is a complaint. The first complaint I heard out of Hudson came in the form of a question: "How is it I worked for, or alongside two male directors that have not been successful in raising money or growing the alumni confidence in giving as successfully as I have, and have not received a promotion?"

It was August of 2015 and Hudson was in the midst of planning the first annual President's Scholarship Gala for Philander Smith College – an event that coincided with the departure of Rodney Parks, the director of development.

"Have you asked the president if he will consider me to replace Rodney as the director of development?"

"Yes. I suggested we consider you for Rodney's replacement, or as a manager of development with a path to become the development director," I responded.

"What did he say?"

"Well, unlike last time I asked him, he didn't respond. The conversation shifted to details of the upcoming gala." I had asked the president in May to consider Hudson for a promotion when the current male director of development told me he was interviewing for a new job. I thought it was appropriate for me to notify the president of the pending vacancy and asked him to give Hudson a chance to move up. At the time, the president responded he "didn't think Hudson was ready." I told Hudson this and she asked for more responsibility.

"What do I have to do to be considered?"

"Just keep performing. Your talent will take you places. The position will be vacant so you can apply for it when it gets posted."

The position was never posted, which was a 'procedural' mistake made by the College. Procedural meaning, at the very least, the College should have posted the job so others would have a fair and equal opportunity to be interviewed for the director of development position.

How did Hudson ever get to the point of filing an EEOC complaint? The lack of opportunity to compete was one reason she filed an EEOC complaint. With her complaint came the question as to how the dispute would be settled. Hudson's complaint maintains she was treated unfairly when it came to promotion consideration. Her male colleagues received the opportunity even though they were less talented. When she asked for her chance to be a director there was absolutely no answer the second time around. It was late August of 2015 and Hudson was handling all three director level assignments I gave her. The planning for the Scholarship Gala was running smoothly. She and another staffer named Rosalyn were working late hours planning for the occasion. They both brought their children to the office in the evening to put in the extra hours required to make the event a success. Rosalyn was a dedicated staffer, making sure we accounted for funds collected for the event. Meanwhile, Hudson was also working double-time towards making the 1877 to Infinity Scholarship campaign a big success by implementing a monthly plan for donations. Even amid doing all of this, Hudson was also planning for a successful homecoming drive for donations. None of the previous male directors handled so much responsibility, with so much success, in the time she had been an employee. She was excited about the challenge.

During the period of gala planning leading up to the event, Hudson questioned me about the College's commitment to honor a procurement decision made with a vendor selected to provide party favors. While planning for the gala, a committee made up of seven people voted to consider vendors to provide party favors. The process involved bidding the opportunity out to local vendors. Once the bids came into the committee of seven (which happened to include me and a great alum of the College, Dr. Charles Donaldson), a vote was held and a bid was accepted. In the next committee meeting, the president approved the decision to select the vendor. Hudson informed the president she would submit the purchase order for signature. Nearly a week later, the purchase order agreement for the vendor had not been signed. Hudson notified me the deadline to produce the party favors was approaching.

Hudson asked, "Has the president returned the signed purchase order agreement? The local vendor, Greek4Life, is awaiting our order."

"I haven't seen it but it may be on his desk. I will check on it again."

Within a day of our conversation, one of our staff members delivered a new purchase order with a new out of state vendor name substituted in place of Greek4Life. The substitute vendor was not on the original list of vendors considered. The president told the staffer to submit the purchase order to accounting. Since the process required a department head sign the purchase order voucher as well, my staffer gave it to me for a signature.

"I have a purchase order for you to sign from the president."

I looked at the voucher and asked, "Did Dr. Donaldson or any of the committee members change the vendor name?"

"No," replied my staffer, "The president changed the vendor name."

I was surprised the vendor change wasn't communicated to anyone on the seven-person committee. I notified Hudson of the change.

"Didn't he approve of the vendor selection in front of the committee? How do I explain to the Greek4Life vendor that he changed his mind? Who is the new vendor he selected?"

"I don't know. This vendor didn't submit a bid for consideration."

I looked closely at the unit cost and discovered the new vendor was offering two cents per unit below the selected vendor.

Hudson questioned the change. "How does an unknown vendor, living in a different part of the country, get notified there was a bid, and miraculously offers a bid just two cents per unit below the winning bid?"

Hudson was worried. How would she explain to seven people that the winning vendor was replaced by an out-of-state vendor without any communication? I wrote the president for an explanation. He was silent. Not just silent for a day or two, but silent nearly seven days after the purchase order was due. I decided to ask the president directly, in a personal meeting referencing the email I sent him.

He explained to me he found a cheaper bid and thought it was within his "purview to select an outside vendor to reduce the price point by two cents."

I laughed, "Mr. President, once the bidding process is voted upon and accepted, the bidding process is closed."

"As President it is my duty to find cheaper ways to make purchases." He responded.

"What good is having a bidding process for vendors if once you get a final bid, you can call a personal friend and give them insider details to beat the winning bid? If this is the way bidding processes work, the College should have simply asked the selected bidder to reduce the price two more cents. We should be honest about the way we operate Mr. President, otherwise people will begin to distrust us. We must operate with integrity."

To Hudson, it was nonsense in having a bidding process if Philander Smith wasn't going to honor its own policy and procedure. Calling someone to share the winning bid after the process was closed, not only violated basic procurement processes, but also took fairness out of the process.

I resubmitted the original purchase order asking the president for a signature, which he then provided. Hudson was back on schedule once the order was submitted. Her duty to observe school procurement policy was admirable. It was clear to me she possessed the right qualities to hold the title of director.

By the end of September 2015, I was in the office 3-4 days a week. I was traveling out of town weekly to help my mother care for my ailing father. Whenever I returned to the office, I would review expenses, make suggestions to Hudson on her upcoming fundraising campaign for homecoming, and work with Rosalyn on reconciliation of donations. Hudson was disappointed she did not get a shot at being the director of development since the job was vacated for over a month; she waited in anticipation for the job to be posted so she could apply. The job was never posted. By early November, on the day of homecoming, Hudson was in full swing. She was delighted to report to me she had met the fundraising goal, and homecoming was underway. On the day of homecoming, I saw Rodney Parks, the previous director of development. We greeted each other and talked about his new job, when he announced to me there was a new director of development. I must have looked shocked because Rodney asked me, "You didn't know?"

"No. I had no idea."

Next Monday at work, there was no sign the rumor was true. No official announcements had been made. Hudson asked me for my opinion.

"I can't believe Cooper was selected over you."

Another staffer in the office responded, "He's been a seminary admissions counselor and a workshop facilitator. He wouldn't know the first thing about fundraising."

Following my next trip out of town, things were different. On November 17, 2015, a formal meeting was held naming Kevin Cooper as the next director of development. Rosalyn told me about it and later Hudson told me as well, and soon others were whispering about it, but I did not see the new director start until December 9, 2015. I was no longer with the

College by December 16, 2015, leaving Hudson to work for a new inexperienced director in the coming new year.

Hudson Termination

On February 22, 2016, I received a call from Hudson saying she had been terminated. She went through the story of her termination in tears with a myriad of thoughts about what happened. She shared why she was so hurt by the unfairness of the College's decision.

"The accusations the College made are not true," she stated.

I thought, "How does a green, inexperienced director without knowledge of fundraising practice decide to terminate a high performing development officer in less than 35 days of being in the job? How does the director of human resources allow the events to take place without perhaps considering a disciplinary warning if one was needed, instead of termination? Why didn't the president of the school intervene? Certainly, he knew she was the best fundraiser the College had, and dumping her endangered her economic security raising a small child. Where were the thoughtful moral leaders in charge of social justice? How does anyone not grasp the impact of the termination outcome?

Hudson's attorney advised her to ask for her job back. The College denied her appeal. This was the first opportunity for moral leadership to redeem itself.

Was the decision to terminate Hudson in line with the College's long-standing tradition of honoring human values? Was there any respect given to her request considering she was a productive performer?

It didn't appear the College was considerate of her situation because they later brought false accusations against her.

Hudson applied for unemployment benefits. The College mounted resistance to unemployment by accusing Hudson of violating a work rule. This certainly would have been easy to explain to all stakeholders: the board, the cabinet, Hudson's friends on campus, and her constituents in the Alumni Association. The unemployment compensation was denied to Hudson. Any hope of a safety net for income was gone. The lack of unemployment benefits created a greater dispute which in turn, generated an emotional flame, which ultimately led to an EEOC complaint. As she recounted her story to me months later, I felt there was an absence of moral decision-making. The College failed to display fairness. It appeared Hudson had no moral voice speaking on her behalf anywhere in leadership, be it in cabinet meetings, in the board room, or on the campus. This woman was all alone. As days went by with her funds running out, ladies at her church helped her find a way to pay her rent. I purchased a tire for her car. She was close to flat broke when she found a job. During this period, she had taken advice from her attorney to file an EEOC charge earlier in the spring when her unemployment had been denied. The complaint process with the EEOC had been initiated but was advancing slowly through the investigation stage. Months had passed when I heard from her concerning the EEOC. This time, she wanted my opinion concerning the EEOC position statement submitted by Philander Smith College. After reading the College's position, I recalled a document I read as a member of the United Methodist Church. The document was titled: "Social Principles of the United Methodist Church" and a passage that particularly struck me was:

"We affirm the right of women to equal treatment in employment, responsibility, promotion, and compensation."

I knew I needed to affirm Hudson's right to equal treatment and promotion even if my friends at the College turned against me.

What if?

We each possess a unique perspective on life. Sometimes our viewpoints are formed by reconsidering context. I thought to myself: What would I think about the Hudson dispute if she was my daughter? Would I feel she had been treated fairly? Would I believe a man with no relevant experience in national fundraising campaigns, no relevant knowledge of basic terms of development should be appointed to run a two-and-a-half million-dollar annual fundraising effort my daughter had been instrumental in building? Would I ignore the fact that the other parts of the position statement addressed an issue Hudson highlighted when no other male director was willing to address it? Did she deserve to be passed up for a director position for having developed the competency to see what others could not see, and the courage to address it? My answer would be "no." No, I would not feel as if my daughter was treated fairly! No, I would not believe the new director capable of running the office he was appointed to by Presidential Proclamation. I would neither ignore nor dismiss my daughter's discovery of shortcomings and oversights that other individuals (in particular, male colleagues) were unwilling to address. When I see women mistreated, I think of my own daughters, needing my support and the support of other family members to overcome the cloaked back room decisions that lead to cases like Hudson's.

What if there was someone courageous enough to stand up to the termination reasons, speaking out about the fairness of the process? What if Hudson had been hired on the merit of her actual documented fundraising performance? It would of course take objectivity to reveal that the reporting was not being accurately portrayed. In my past role, I had presented reports to the College on matters which needed to be addressed. Matters Hudson raised. Did anyone recall past board reports? Did anyone inquire about cabinet reports I had submitted? Would there be any objective stakeholders with a moral conviction to search for truth, rather than listen to biased insiders seeking to protect the image of the College, or their personal position and title? The "what if" game was tiring. No one would come forward to dispel the misrepresentations in the position statement. And without the truth, no one would believe Hudson. She would have to seek vindication on her own, without protection from the innuendo and rumor of backroom meetings where anything could be said about her without grounds. Hudson was a good colleague and is a good person. I don't know if anyone in power on the campus ever thought about her in these terms: good, honest, dedicated, mission-oriented, kind, resourceful, and courageous. It was her courage, her determination to speak the truth, that got Hudson in trouble. She spoke truth to power, and power retaliated.

In a past career

Years ago, in a different career, I was walking down the hallway of my employer when I overheard two women talking about a male manager who would give unwanted massages, blow kisses, and ask female employees out for dates. Flirting at work in some environments is common. Managers touching, kissing and soliciting direct subordinates is undeniably inappropriate and can be illegal. I trailed the women to their department to ascertain who their manager was. What manager on earth would risk their career conducting themselves in a manner that clearly violated our harassment policy? It was troubling to me, however, that no one had reported harassment. Fortunately, a fellow co-worker solved the mystery for me. She saw me drift by the front door of the department and caught up with me. "Mr. Duvall," she said, "May I come to your office on lunch break? I need to share something with you. It's about our department." I told her to call my secretary, Angie, and make an appointment. Late in the afternoon, I met with Ms. Smith. Her story was unbelievable; not in the sense that I did not believe her, but in the sense that it was so incredible it could have made for a soap opera. Ms. Smith told me there were four women in her department who were being harassed. One of them was even a supervisor. Their manager frequently asked the women about their sex lives on the weekend, sometimes to the extent of suggesting he would be willing to spend time with them if they were lonely or needed a date. The story painted a vivid and disturbing picture of female employees that experienced caressing and whispering while they sat at their work desks with the manager leaning over their shoulders making advances. I asked Ms. Smith if she experienced this treatment personally.

"Yes, but my manager pursued the other women more aggressively because I would make comments about how uncomfortable I felt, creating more attention in the moment than the manager wanted." she responded.

I asked, "Why hasn't someone reported this to human resources or to your next level managers?"

Her answer was simple. "We don't know who we can trust. Our manager is a personal friend of the division vice president who hired him. It's not unusual to see the two of them together. It's intimidating to know our manager has that type of connection – he flaunts it."

"What do you mean he flaunts it?" I asked.

"He reminds us of his relationship with upper management. He talks about having attended college with him. He invites him down to see the department. They laugh and talk about non-work-related events. If you see such a relationship you think twice about saying anything. But there is another factor making us hesitant to say anything. Our supervisor who has to report to our manager, receives the same type of harassing treatment. She has told us to focus on our jobs and not rock the boat because our jobs are more important. She is afraid too!"

I didn't know where to start. "Why are you telling me this now?"

"Mr. Duvall, I have a new job offer with another company. I will be leaving in two weeks. Someone needs to say something and frankly, I had to wait until the right moment to tell you. One day, in the cafeteria, I met you and sensed you cared about people; but even then, I needed a couple more interactions with you before I could trust you. It is hard to trust management when you have seen people get railroaded in their career. Today, I could tell you didn't know what was going on because you walked right past our manager without speaking to him in the hallway," she said.

I nodded and chuckled. I was on reconnaissance. If the manager didn't recognize me as an executive, it made it easier for me to go unnoticed while I learned more about our work culture. I was sympathetic to her plight and to the plight of her female colleagues. I would need their trust, so the next step was gaining it – but it put all of us in jeopardy.

"Look, I have a way to get this on a fast track with a substantial effort to investigate your complaint. I have heard the story from you, and I have heard a partial story in the hallway. I need you to tell the supervisor that you have disclosed to me what is going on in the department. Surely, she is looking for you by now." Smith had been in my office for more than thirty minutes.

"Call your supervisor from my office phone. My caller ID will pop up. Tell your supervisor to come up to my office right away."

She agreed and within a few minutes Ms. Smith's supervisor was in my office. Ms. Smith's supervisor was an experienced employee with a record of good performance. She seemed comfortable about coming to my office. I excused Ms. Smith so I could talk privately with Ms. Jones. Ms. Jones told me the same story Ms. Smith told me. The flirtatiousness, the inappropriate touching, the leering looks down the blouses of female co-workers; all of it was substantiated without Ms.

Jones knowing exactly what Ms. Smith told me. When I got to the heart of the matter, tears welled up in her eyes.

"Why didn't you report this to human resources? Why did you put up with it? Why did you discourage others from reporting it?"

Ms. Jones was clear. "My husband and I have a blended family. We were married a year ago. Together we have five children. He was laid off six months ago, and we cannot afford to be without my income. The other women are in similar situations. Some are in single income homes, caring for their families. We cannot risk losing our jobs over a complaint. My manager knows people in high places. It's scary."

I said, "Listen, I have a way for you to get protection by making me accountable, but I need you to cooperate in getting every single possible complainant to my office."

Ms. Jones used my office phone and called employees one at a time to write down their stories. They were not alerted to the reason until they arrived and I interviewed two more (four of the six) and I then told Ms. Jones to report the interviews to the company ethics hotline and state she's making sexual harassment complaints against her manager. The executive vice president needed to be present for the report. The report goes to an outside party that transcribes it to a notification which goes to internal audit. The process was a control our company put in place to be sure three separate branches of our company were notified independently, so no one unit could suppress a report. The corporate legal department, the internal audit department, and the corporate employee relations department would be notified and then one of the branches would investigate. My head of employee relations was notified by internal audit. I must have looked a bit sheepish when one of my directors asked me why I didn't just tell the employees to report it to human resources. I explained how the employees were leery of reporting anything because of the manager's senior management connections, and potential ability to suppress the story. The ethics in the workplace hotline protected the company from internal management interference. Hotlines are free of personal agendas that corrupt the process of reporting wrong doing. My mission was to free the women from their fear of being terminated for speaking up. The outcome of the investigation by objective parties ultimately worked. The manager was removed from the job after seven women, and two men corroborated the complaint.

Most companies don't have such a system. All investigations are reported to the same people who have control of the story, or control of the outcomes. When moral leadership elements of fairness, respect, and honesty prevail, the likelihood of a complaint based upon misrepresentations of an employee's character is less likely to occur. Improper disciplinary actions, discrimination, or unfair terminations are less likely to result. All of this relates back to Hudson's case because her charge suggested an absence of moral leadership because the "facts" used in her EEOC position statement were not fair, respectful, or honest. It wasn't fair to put an inexperienced male in the position she was qualified to fill. The comments about her behavior not resolving were not truthful of her professional success, and despite what the position statement read, she positively had national campaign fundraising experience. Moral leadership looks for truth, fights for truth, and stands for truth. Moral leadership is essential in a world in which the term 'justice' is used freely in conversations, tag lines and speeches to raise money. Moral leadership is informed by actions that fight for fairness, diminish fear, treat others with respect, support honest partners, invite open investigations, and have no tolerance for unethical investigations. There was something unethical in the way the story about Hudson was presented. Misleading statements transformed the entire document into an attack on Hudson rather than a defense against a claim. It was absolutely essential I affirmed her right to "equal treatment in employment, in responsibility, in promotion and compensation."

CHAPTER FOUR

Retaliation

"Man must evolve for all human conflict a method which
rejects revenge, aggression and retaliation.
The foundation of such a method is love."
—Martin Luther King, Jr.

The College's discriminatory acts were devoid of a moral conscience. Through her faith in God, Hudson sought to repel the aggression hurled her way by the College's actions. The College she loved so dearly did not love her back. In his Nobel acceptance speech of 1964, Martin Luther King, Jr., opined that love, not aggression or retaliation, was the foundation for a method towards living in peace. For nearly three years, Hudson had no peace in her fight to be heard and compensated for the discriminatory decisions by the College. As a Christian, Hudson made it clear to me the retaliatory actions of the College did not demonstrate "Christian Love" as pronounced in their creative storytelling in the position statement. One of Hudson's legal charges was that Philander

Smith College retaliated against her for making a complaint of discrimination. Hudson charged she was terminated for complaining about loss of a promotional opportunity; therefore, her termination was considered retaliation. But complaining is not the only reason a person can be targeted for retaliation. A 'witness' that corroborates in an interview about witnessing discrimination can also be the victim of retaliation for engaging in what should be a protected activity. For example, in a recent conversation, a claimant explained to me that she had the support of two women who would vouch for her if she voiced her complaint only to lose both of their voices of support after she was terminated. The claimant made it clear she believed her witnesses lost their resolve to testify because her employer has historically terminated, demoted or underpaid women for dissenting. Her witnesses dropped out because of fear! Fear of reprisal is what the EEOC calls a 'chilling' effect. To further elaborate, I cite directly from the EEOC website and their article concerning examples of retaliation:

What is Retaliation and Why It Matters?

A manager may not fire, demote, harass or otherwise "retaliate" against an individual for filing a complaint of discrimination, participating in a discrimination proceeding, or otherwise opposing discrimination. The same laws that prohibit discrimination based on race, color, sex, religion, national origin, age, disability and genetic information also prohibit retaliation against individuals who oppose unlawful discrimination or participate in an employment discrimination proceeding.

It is important to understand how retaliation manifests and to prevent it from occurring. If retaliation for such activities were permitted, it would have a chilling effect upon the willingness of individuals to speak out against employment discrimination or to participate in the EEOC's administrative process or other employment discrimination proceedings. Thus, EEO practitioners must work diligently with managers to ensure that retaliation is not permitted in the workplace.

It is obvious that the cause and effect of interpersonal conflicts can potentially implicate a legal process. This is particularly apparent with retaliation law because the legal standard requires an examination of the behavior after the allegation. The standard for proving a retaliation claim requires showing that the manager's action might deter a reasonable person from opposing discrimination or participating in the EEOC complaint process.

Examples from past cases provide instructive illustrations of typical retaliatory behavior:

In a recent case, an employee who had filed several unsuccessful EEO complaints, subsequently sought promotions within the organization. The employee learned that her manager had placed information about the previous EEO proceedings in her personnel file and communicated that the employee had filed several complaints when contacted for reference checks. The EEOC found that the statements made during the reference check were retaliatory and further that the EEO information placed in the employee's personnel file was unnecessary and hindered her promotional opportunities.

Similarly, another recent case involved an employee who claimed that she was discriminated against during the promotional interview process. Two of the three interview panelists were managers involved in current or previous EEO complaints by the employee and one of the panelists attempted to influence the selection process by asking a question that paralleled a previous conflict between the panelist and the employee. A witness reported that he had heard the manager make the statement, "I don't get mad, I get even" in reference to employees who make discrimination claims. EEOC found that the selection process was tainted by retaliatory conduct and ordered the agency to promote the employee.

In another example, EEOC found retaliation partly based on the fact that the employee was refused use of a government vehicle. In this case, the manager's reaction to the employee's EEO complaint was to take away a perk (i.e., use of the government car), while another coworker was allowed continued use of the vehicle. While the manager had the discretion to allocate the use of the vehicle and other "perks," retaliation can be established if it is shown to be more likely than not that the discretionary decision was based upon a retaliatory motive.

While close temporal proximity between the EEO allegation and the manager's action can be a key factor in establishing the retaliatory motive, there have been cases in which years have passed and other evidence established that the employee's earlier EEO activities motivated the manager's action. Even absent suspicious timing, other relevant facts may include verbal or written statements; comparative evidence that a similarly situated employee was treated differently; falsity of the employer's proffered reason for the adverse action; or any other evidence from which an inference of retaliatory intent might be drawn.

In a final example, EEOC found that management was openly hostile towards an employee's protected EEO activity. Specifically, the employee's manager described the employee's discrimination allegations as "unprofessional,"

> *and his higher-level manager found them "highly offensive" and "bad for morale." During the subsequent EEO proceeding, coworkers revealed an overall feeling of distrust and concern about the employee after his initial complaint. EEOC noted that the first-level manager saw this growing tension, but failed to ensure that coworkers understood and respected the employee's right to file a complaint.*

Based upon this information, Hudson likely had another challenge facing her: lack of empathy or care for her plight. According to Hudson and confirmed by my research, people on campus knew about her claims. Hudson stated others on campus had already been told that Kevin Cooper bragged about her termination. Worse, however, and something she could not control, was the public relations information suggesting she deserved her fate. Imagine the courage it would take for someone on campus to become a witness, exposed to the scrutiny of the culture on campus. I thought Hudson did not stand a chance of getting witnesses to come forward if she called for help. This is how effective 'retaliation' can be when employer culture is primed to create narratives like the one in the College's position statement. How then, will anyone challenge and prevent it from happening? To any woman? All victims must take the risk if they speak up. All witnesses must also take the risk to speak up; moreover, anyone believing in justice must stand up. But not alone.

According to fiscal year 2017 EEOC statistics, retaliation claims outnumbered any other charge made by claimants: more than race, more than sex, more than disability, age or religion. Retaliation stands atop all charges. I hope there are victims, witnesses, or empathetic sojourners who will realize that a true opportunity to promote justice might be birthed through a women's movement focused on seeking a commitment of change on campus. Fear of telling the truth, speaking the truth; or living the truth; should not be a part of the campus culture. Hudson possessed no fear of speaking truth to power – a fact that was made evident on four memorable occasions:

The first event occurred in the Spring of 2015. Hudson asked the chief financial officer (CFO) of the institution about a change in reported endowment numbers on a statement prepared for a family member of the endowed honoree she had been servicing. Hudson was being a good fiduciary agent of the College when she asked the CFO of the College about the error in reporting. The administrator was unsettled by her questions and became contentious with her. While the meeting ended amicably, it was clear that Hudson had ruffled some feathers by trying to help clear up matters for a donor family. Nothing discriminatory occurred in this exchange; yet, I perceived Hudson's investigation was not well received by the CFO.

The second occasion during which Hudson spoke truth to power occurred in July of 2015, during an alumni executive committee meeting of the National Alumni Association. Representatives of each alumni chapter were on a conference call. During the call, one of the officers made a motion to cancel a previous donation commitment made by the entire convention body of the National Alumni Association held earlier in April. The commitment was to place funds in the 1877 to Infinity Scholarship Fund. The purpose of the cancellation was to accommodate a request by the College to move the funds toward supporting the new President's Scholarship Gala. Despite the fact that moving the funds to the Scholarship Gala would actually help Hudson's effort as the Chairperson of the event, Hudson and Ms. Erma Williams objected to moving the funds on the grounds that the alumni by-laws restricted overturning a vote of the convention body. Hudson simply spoke the truth. The meeting took place on a Sunday evening. On Tuesday, July 21, the president somehow noted Hudson's objection on the call, even though he was not a part of the decision at the time Hudson's objection was raised. The president suggested Hudson be terminated from her job with the College. I objected to the suggestion to terminate Hudson for two reasons. First, she was not attending a College sponsored meeting; therefore, she was not acting in her capacity as an employee of the College. The alumni association has a separate legal identification from the College, represented by a separate charter, a separate set of by-laws, a separate executive officer structure, and a separate 501(c)3 number. Second, Hudson was the leading fundraiser for the College. It did not make sense to terminate the school's best fundraiser for such a small reason. Hudson would ultimately raise significant amounts of funds for the College leading up to the gala and to the 2015 homecoming. Nonetheless, her apparent willingness to hold to the alumni chapter by-laws emboldened the president to seek her dismissal. This request by the president was not discriminatory; however, it signaled that Hudson was on the president's radar to be dismissed.

The pattern of speaking truth to power continued into late July of 2015 when Hudson asked if a purchase order (PO) agreed upon by the president had been signed for processing. When she discovered the PO had been altered to go to an unrecognized vendor, she objected to the inappropriate change and asked me to meet with the president on her behalf. Her point, and my opinion as well, was that the College should live up to its word and not give away insider information (the amount of the winning financial bid). Hudson's position was based upon sound procurement policy and honest dealing. Once again, Hudson was challenging the president on sound footing in the interest of honest dealing.

The inciting event that lead up to an act of discrimination occurred November 17, 2015. It was an August 2015 request for a promotion by Hudson. When I explained there had not been an affirmative response from the president, she challenged me directly, articulating her successes in her position compared to the men. While I assured her that the College would give her a chance to compete when the position became open, she was floored by the November 17, 2015, announcement of the selection of a male with no relevant experience. She was vocal to others about the slight. She complained about the decision. I believe this was the period in which her situation reverberated across the campus with one cabinet member even suggesting she come work in a different department with him. It wasn't long after this slight that Hudson was terminated by the College. It was a sad, rapid fall from a promising career for a woman who sought to excel while benefiting others, in the field of her choice. Hudson's attorney would argue her complaint was promotion discrimination and her termination, was retaliation.

> *A manager may not fire, demote, harass or otherwise "retaliate" against an individual for filing a complaint of discrimination, participating in a discrimination proceeding, or otherwise opposing discrimination. The same laws that prohibit discrimination based on race, color, sex, religion, national origin, age, disability and genetic information also prohibit retaliation against individuals who oppose unlawful discrimination or participate in an employment discrimination proceeding.*
> —EEOC

CHAPTER FIVE

Dialogue

"Your silence is consent."
—Plato

The help Hudson needed in understanding the EEOC process was a revelation in terms of understanding what claimants go through, from the day they file their charge, to the day the EEOC closes their charge. Hudson wasn't aware the EEOC would ask her to prepare a reply to the College's response. Her efforts to interview me based upon my knowledge of our shared work environment was awkward for both of us. She was asking the right questions about my knowledge of the male development directors but she wasn't sure of her writing. I helped her edit and make revisions in order to best communicate her position. As I asked her questions, I became her scribe. The final version of her reply was a combination of my and her draft. It was essential she submitted her "truth," so I questioned her, reminding her to go find documents, emails, screen shots, memos, letters and anything else related to her statements in order to support her claim. I also gave her my testimony as it related to what I knew, hoping Philander Smith's attorneys would find discovery linked to her claim. I wanted the College to find the truth in their own records. I wanted Hudson and the school to have a dialogue about the case and resolve their differences, ending the matter in an EEOC mediation. The College wouldn't budge.

Lack of communication separates people. Outright refusal to speak polarizes all parties involved. The College's decision not to mediate was detrimental to their case without the College understanding the consequences. Hudson filed her lawsuit and half way through the process, the College was still lagging in fundraising because their former employee had an influential base of donors back away from giving. I know this because members of the alumni association talked among themselves freely about fundraising shortages. Finances were reeling and the College needed stronger fundraising efforts. Bottom line: Not having Hudson hurt their cash flow.

In December of 2017, I received a call from Hudson's lawyer informing me I would be subpoenaed to testify in the civil rights case between Hudson and Philander Smith College. The call was straight forward and businesslike, but not unexpected. The voice on the other end was someone I knew from years past when we both worked together in a corporate setting. As was her custom, Melanie greeted me courteously.

"Hi C.J., this is Melanie."

"Hello Counselor," I said pleasantly. I have a high regard for Melanie based on past experience. She is one of the most genuine people I have ever met.

"I am sure by now you know we are moving toward a subpoena of your testimony?"

"Yep. Gemessia warned me months ago."

"I am thinking of scheduling you sometime in January. How does your schedule look during the second week?"

"Okay. I think I can arrange my schedule to be free most of the month after the first week if you let me know."

"You will need to retain any and all records related to the federal complaint, as well as refrain from talking about the case."

"I understand Melanie. When do I get subpoenaed?"

"Not sure yet." Melanie's voice moved to a more serious tone. "Despite our history, you need to be aware I cannot treat you any different than the other males. Gemessia said she asked you for a promotion. It makes you one of the guys I will have to challenge."

"I respect it. I just want to tell the truth."

Once the call ended, I sighed heavily, not because I feared testifying, but because I knew the complaint could have been avoided with open dialogue, and without the College enduring a short-term financial loss. Philander Smith College had mounting legal fees because of the defense the College maintained. The case was still open and the potential for further financial impact to the College was growing.

The cost of filing a lawsuit

Hudson was fortunate to have a contingency agreement with an attorney; without it she may not have pursued her claim with the EEOC or pursued a lawsuit against Philander Smith College. A contingency lawyer takes on or shares the burden of the cost related to pursuing a judgment against a defendant. The financial costs incurred can be staggering, considering it could take nearly 18 months to 2 years for a case to make its way to court not to mention the prospect for an appeal.. Consider the following list of possible out-of-pocket expenses for a plaintiff:

1. A one-hour introductory advisory session with an attorney.

2. A second set of sessions with the attorney if selected after the advisory session.

3. Time and expense to gather information, evidence, or materials useful to the attorney in writing and filing the initial charge complaint.

4. Possible administrative fees associated with the back office copying and cataloging materials.

5. Possible fees from the attorney to prepare for an EEOC mediation if there is a mediation.

6. Attorney's fees to write a claimant reply to the defendant's response statement (this is where I helped Hudson save money by giving her advice and editing support which saved her 4-6 hours of billing).

7. Fees to have the attorney write the complaint for a lawsuit.

8. The filing fee for the lawsuit.

9. Conversations with the attorney to advance the case.

10. Conversations between the plaintiff's attorney and the defendant's attorney billed to the represented parties.

11. The cost of writing or responding to motions to dismiss (as Philander Smith College attempted two motions for dismissal).

12. The administrative costs related to the additional steps connected to the motions.

13. The cost of attorneys to qualify or screen potential witnesses via phone calls.

14. The cost to subpoena witnesses.

15. The cost of depositions (questioning) of witnesses.

16. The clerk cost of taking and preparing the interrogatories.

17. The cost of reviewing interrogatories with clients.

18. The cost of reviewing, documenting and cataloging production (discovery or evidence).

19. The cost of creating exhibits to be used in depositions.

20. The administrative fees for unusual requests.

21. Attorney's fees for preparing and appearing before a magistrate for mediation (if the sides agree to mediate).

22. The cost of travel to depose a witness (or) arrange for a taped deposition of a witness.

23. The cost of pre-trial preparation, inclusive of writing case summaries for the judge.

24. The cost of technology tools to present and display evidence in the courtroom.

25. The cost of 3-4 full days of court proceedings.

By the time their trial date arrived, both parties could have spent close to $100,000, each. If Hudson won at trial seeking punitive damages, the amount of money for the case would rise three-fold. Theoretically, the entire cost of this case could be close to $300,000 or more. I believed Hudson would prevail; and Philander Smith College (and its insurance company) would have lost time and money on a case that was lost the day they made a discriminatory decision.

There are other costs in this case, one which I have mentioned briefly, which are the lost donations from the productivity of a capable fundraiser. I estimated about $500,000 was lost in fundraising mid-way through the case. It would be substantially more due to the publicity after the jury trial. The College wasn't thinking – unless they were trying to bluff Hudson.

The worst cost of all was incalculable: emotional and mental distress. I cannot quantify what I observed in Hudson's behavior. I can describe how often she called in tears in the early stages of this long ordeal. Later Hudson moved from tears to a quiet resolve, determined to continue to challenge the number of false statements made in the position statement. I could feel her disappointment with the school's leadership. I could feel her struggling to maintain her confidence in the values of fairness, goodness, and honesty. Friends and family encouraged her along the way. People gave her gift cards, money for her car repairs and meals. I used my Goodyear credit card to help her buy a tire. My wife and I rented a house to Hudson for her and her daughter. Her sudden termination by the College was presented to the unemployment compensation office as a termination for "cause," resulting in the cancellation of special insurance she carried to protect her from catastrophic job loss (like a layoff). The school's decision wreaked havoc on her professional, personal, and economic life and no judge or jury in the world would understand how to measure what Hudson had to withstand. A board member, clergy person, or administrator did little to stop the dispute. Every single person associated with the College administration was shackled by a legal process absent of any dialogue.

Resolution to Disputes

I believed the College should have tried to resolve the dispute with Hudson. They had several opportunities: (1) Before her termination, (2) during her appeal process, (3) in the unemployment hearing, and (4) in the EEOC process. Unfortunately, dispute resolution is not a core strength of the College; otherwise they would not have spent so much time and attorney's fees working against Hudson, which in a sense was working against justice. Here are mediation techniques that have worked in my past experiences and could have been considered in this case:

1. Reassignment. Hudson didn't want to work for an inexperienced manager. She had seven years of experience raising large amounts of money. She wanted to be a director.

2. Reinstatement. After Hudson was terminated, the College could have reinstated her after she appealed. She raised more than $200,000 per year as a development officer and was continuing to grow into a strong fundraiser. She could have easily reached the million-dollar peak because she had a history of writing grants, working on national campaigns, supporting scholarship drives and leading homecoming fundraisers. Those different elements combined, would have been a huge benefit and advantage to the College.

3. Mediation. The College couldn't bring themselves to reinstate Hudson after termination. They still could have mediated a small settlement for $25,000, closed the charge and moved on quietly in 2016, instead the College wasted thousands of dollars.

Speedy resolution of employment disputes can save parties from embarrassing discoveries; for example, there were public records that contradicted defense statements made by the College in their position statement. I was absolutely embarrassed for the College when I saw the written contradictions in their defense. It appeared to be a costly effort for them. Hudson was fortunate enough to have a law firm take her case on contingency in her pursuit of a fair resolution; otherwise, it would have been impossible for her to afford a case. I think the College was betting on her to fold. Hudson stood firm. While the College was focused on the legal fight, the real shame was that the College failed to think of kindness, humanitarian impact, and goodwill. Why attempt to further victimize an existing victim? If the College was to represent spirituality (one of Philander Smith College's timeless human values), why make Hudson a victim at all? The College talked about justice to promote their "Justice 2.0" program, but offered no refuge to Hudson from injustice. The College's position was parallel to an observation made by ESPN journalist Jamele Hill when discussing problems at her alma mater, Michigan State University. Hill stated: "Protection of image, of order, of title, of program often becomes more important than protecting the actual student…" In *Hudson vs Philander Smith College*, it is an employee and alumna of Philander Smith College that was left unprotected by the College of "social justice."

Considering Hudson's plight, I could not be silent in the face of her plea for help. History and current events inform all of us that silence in the face of injustice is consent. Silence is not an acceptable answer to injustice. Silence to injustice is the reason why this country had and has a civil rights movement, a Black Lives Matter movement, a #MeToo movement, and a gay rights movement (and maybe even a new gun violence movement that changes our political governance). Silence is why Philander Smith College is embroiled in one of the biggest justice fights they have had in years. In my opinion, when it came to Hudson, they were fighting on the wrong side of justice and lacked the competence to know it.

Conclusion

The College, like many employers, defaulted to the use of employment practices liability insurance. Somehow, the College was convinced they had a strong defense, as perhaps was their law firm. I am not sure if either of them truly understood the lack of evidence; or, if the College simply decided to use their liability insurance in order to let their lawyers pull a rabbit out of the proverbial hat. I believe their strategy was to see how far the case could go on the strength of their law firm and not because they believed they could win. Such a strategy yielded temporary financial protection for the College and provided the law firm steady billing; however, it did not yield a thoughtful evaluation of ethics like speaking truth. What the insurance company couldn't know was that the College could have diffused the employment dispute in September 2015, by interviewing Hudson for the job. A promotion or selection decision was not required. Instead, in my opinion, the College inflamed the situation by fabricating a false position statement intended to harm Hudson.

Inflaming the situation by attacking the victim was not an act of benevolence rather, it was an arrogant stance taken by an institution with power. When Hudson received a right to sue notification from the EEOC, it led to her filing a civil rights lawsuit against her alma mater. The rollercoaster of *Hudson versus Philander Smith College* left the starting platform with the employer clutching its insurance policy, and the plaintiff brandishing her truth. Hudson was in the better position.

CHAPTER SIX

Was It Worth It?

"It is easy to talk about justice. It is harder to achieve justice."
—C.J. Duvall, Jr.

"Speaking the truth is the most powerful tool we all have."
—Oprah Winfrey

More than two years after Hudson filed an EEOC charge against her alma mater, and one year after she filed a federal complaint in *"Hudson versus Philander Smith College,"* the case ended quietly. It never went to court. Throughout her long ordeal, public records reveal Philander Smith College filed motions to dismiss Hudson's complaint. It did not work. A federal judge denied the motions to dismiss, leaving the College to either face off in the court room or settle her case. The College elected to settle the case out of court. No one will ever know the outcome of the private session between the two parties. I believe it was a logical decision for the institution and the insurance company to settle. The College would have had to raise more money to finance their defense. Furthermore, by the time of trial, Hudson would have presented a mountain of evidence of screen shots, backed up personal files, emails from her employer, and searchable public evidence from the Internet. Hudson would have also subpoenaed the fundraising records for the period during which she was employed, in order to demonstrate how little the male directors raised in comparison to her own productivity. While the College's story appeared believable, the inconsistencies in their account did not stand up to scrutiny.

The legal implication of Hudson's approach to seeking justice can be summed up in a single observation: Now that claimants can have access to a defendant's position statement, attorneys will need to be more careful not to be swooned by a charismatic client story too good to be true without first looking for substantive evidence. The January 1, 2016, EEOC policy change allowing claimants to see how employers respond to charges helped Hudson identify the College's weak narrative, motivating her to advance her challenge. Hudson's story, ending in a quiet settlement, complicates matters for future plaintiffs. A trial would have fully opened Hudson's matter to the public via a courtroom account likely ending up in the press. The College protected its image by settling Hudson's case, leaving one remaining area of investigation: the question of integrity.

The question of integrity

Is the virtue of integrity dead in our society? The story submitted in the position statement by Philander Smith College failed the integrity test. Possibly four people in management shared viewpoints, opinions, and decisions that were narrated in the position statement. Hudson's challenge to the College was, in reality, a challenge to the management team's integrity – the same team that approved the position statement submission to the U.S. Equal Employment Opportunity Commission. Hudson called parts of their position statement "lies." For the College, settling the lawsuit ended the financial threat of a large award at trial; however, the true dilemma was the unexplained lack of integrity inherent in the story. I cite fifteen examples from my prepared testimony:

1. December 2014: During the time I worked for the College, I met with the UNCF. Kevin Cooper was relationship manager for the UNCF, conducting workshops for the Gates Millennium Scholars program. He was not a national fundraiser as stated by the College. I expected to share this information under subpoena.

2. Hudson had worked nearly 7 years in fundraising. The male candidate selected by "Presidential

Proclamation" over Hudson did not have relevant, or superior fundraising experience.

3. The College failed to explain Hudson was the leading fundraiser in the Office of Institutional Advancement in 2015. Electronic drafts of notes for staff meetings, cabinet meetings, and board meetings were saved in backed-up files on the College's server. The College did not realize objective evidence of Hudson's success would dwarf the fundraising records of the previous two male directors; yet, she was not given an opportunity to compete for the open position. I suspect no one searched for this evidence, except perhaps her 2015 performance evaluation.

4. The College donor database maintained fundraising records for 2013-2015. The database would provide additional evidence that not only showed Hudson outperformed two male directors, but also contradicted a letter Hudson received from the College stating she was unqualified for the position of director. She was unequivocally qualified by virtue of her years of experience, but more so, for results.

5. There were several potential witnesses available to present testimony on Hudson's leadership displayed during the first annual Scholarship Gala where she

oversaw a committee of seven people and several other volunteers, to raise over $300,000 in a single night. During the planning of the event, she encountered a problem with a procurement decision which I related in a story told in Chapter 3. She was hardworking and steadfast during the Gala's event planning process. The same steadfast attitude carried over into her lawsuit of discrimination against the College. The College's position statement totally ignored Hudson's professional accomplishments and success as a fundraiser.

6. Hudson and I identified stewardship concerns the male directors never identified and tracked. Hudson questioned important financial management discrepancies. I reported the stewardship concerns to the administration in hopes management would take it as a sign that fellow staff members were prepared to help the College clean up evident problems.

7. News articles and press releases dating back two plus years contained information pre-dating the College's story that claimed the newly selected male director's national fundraising campaign success.

8. During the time of Hudson's employment dispute and after her EEOC complaint, a fraternal brother of the president and a trustee of the College met with

me in a private lunch meeting in Batesville, Arkansas. More than a year after Hudson's termination, the trustee shared information concerning mismanagement of College funds and low fundraising which, according to him was at an all-time low. The content of his confession vindicated Hudson's complaint that endowment balances were not properly reported, and she was the better fundraiser. I was prepared to testify as to the name of the trustee, share the meeting minutes and share the name of the witness who was present during the meeting in Batesville.

9. The College attempted to justify Hudson's termination by claiming she violated a contract signature policy. It sounded plausible; however, such a policy was not published, discussed, enforced or used in the Office of Institutional Advancement. Furthermore, not a single male had ever been terminated for such an act, much less reprimanded. In April of 2016, the College sent me separate correspondence signed by the president, seemingly in conflict with the story that the College told the EEOC.

10. In February of 2016, I was not employed with the College when Hudson was dismissed and she took leave from the College to care for her mother while she was employed with the College. She told me about

the medical issue and I told her to call her Human Resources department to get the proper Family Medical Leave Act (FMLA) paperwork. She received an email from Human Resources directing her management team to adhere to the FMLA rules. I told her to keep every piece of correspondence that came from the College. She followed my recommendation. It turned out to be a crucial part of evidence she planned to use to support a retaliation complaint which was another facet of her discrimination lawsuit. If Hudson had not retained the communication from the College, her complaint would have been swept under the rug.

11. Hudson told me about a disciplinary document used against her in the unemployment hearing. It was something she had never seen before, meaning she thought it was created after her termination. I advised her to ask for electronic discovery of the "creation" date in the file properties. The finding would not have proved discrimination, but it would have demonstrated the lack of integrity for creating a piece of evidence manufactured after Hudson was terminated. A version of the document was left on a copier machine at the College. The document was being drafted and created nearly a full week after Hudson's departure!

I was prepared to testify how evidence like the document could be forensically dated.

12. The College stated Hudson's "behavior and attitude with her supervisors did not resolve..." The reference compared an alleged incident in 2013 with a single alleged incident in 2016, on the day of her termination. Factually, the statement on page 4 of the position statement was not true in 2014 or 2015. Hudson was the top performer. Two entire years of exceptional performance was not mentioned when she worked for an entirely different management team.

13. The College remarked with unequivocal certainty that Hudson had no experience on national fundraising campaigns. The statement would be easily debunked with my testimony and the testimony of my friend Ron Newsome, the former president of the National Alumni Association, citing Hudson's Last Mile Campaign liaison responsibilities during the national capital campaign.

14. The assertion that Hudson's "behavior and attitude with supervisors did not resolve," would have been countered with truthful substance. I told Hudson to subpoena her performance evaluation; 'thank you' notes; cards and letters of congratulations from

leading donors, and records indicating her stellar fundraising performance to account for the 'missing' period.

15. Finally, the statement the College made concerning the male director's 'significant fundraising experience' could be debunked by the public information on the Internet, witnesses at the UNCF, the director of alumni affairs, and of course, a review of the male director's resume (which would have indicated his experience was heavily weighted with admissions and recruiting experience).

In summary, the College attempted to discredit Hudson without evidence. The attempt to discredit Hudson lacked two important virtues: *kindness and integrity*. There was nothing kind in the way Hudson was mistreated at termination and there was nothing honest in the way that her story was presented to the EEOC, to the College's law firm, or to the insurance company. I am not sure if the effort was worth it to the College. Hudson's contribution to fundraising for Philander Smith College was roughly valued at $200,000 – $250,000, annually. The College lost at least $600,000 of her productivity by the time it settled out of court. The value of the settlement is confidential and there is no record of how much the College paid Hudson or how much legal expense the insurance company suffered in settling the case for Philander Smith College.

The total cost for the insurance company was likely six figures. Whatever the cost, it may have caused the College to malinger from its own self-inflicted wound. They could not afford to call their witnesses and go to trial. Was the effort of the College to fight Hudson worth it?

Epilogue

The truth in a story is never one-sided. It is never just a lawyer's voice, a president's voice, or a cabinet member's voice that makes it valid. The truth in a story includes the victim's voice. In the Hudson story there is the challenge of hearing the victim's voice. We will probably never hear the voice of the victim in the *Hudson versus Philander Smith College* case as a settlement document forbids the plaintiff from sharing details. In a review of this book, a long-time friend offered up a powerful opinion concerning Hudson's possible settlement. My friend stated: "A settlement is not justice because her case never made it to trial to allow the process of justice to play out."

Getting to trial perhaps would have extended the process towards a just decision for Hudson; however, I think the College community is missing something far more important than a court decision when it comes to fair and just outcomes. I believe the reason Hudson filed a lawsuit was because she believed she was discriminated against and the College's defense was lacking. I think the College was not honest in their dealings with Hudson. Integrity in the selection process was missing, bringing ruinous consequences to both parties. The College lost thousands of dollars in income Hudson formerly helped to raise. Hudson lost sleep and peace of mind. An adjudicated "settlement" did not address the loss on either side. The true loss is the brokenness in the community as a result of this case. There was no leadership from any quarter to address it. The brokenness existed in four elements: (1) process and decision-making lacked integrity; (2) there was a failure to model moral leadership for cabinet, faculty, staff, and students; (3) there was an absence of restorative justice; and (4) there was a missed opportunity for spiritual reconciliation. This book covered the first element of brokenness by demonstrating "process and decision making" lacked integrity and led to the Hudson case. This first element needs to be addressed within the College to avoid more Hudson's. The other three elements are future motifs of exploration.

The second element, "modeling moral leadership," refers to the actions and decisions made within the College administration which serve as a "training" ground to those within the College community. What is the College modeling in the way of moral leadership when it is allowed to treat Hudson and others in such a way? What is the College saying when position statements are easily supported without factual evidence? Is there a concern for the well-being of faculty, staff, and students who are exposed to unjust, unfair, and inappropriate decisions? Has the College recognized they may be training a generation to support and model the behavior of creating narratives that scuttle the truth? Are faculty and staff learning to ignore injustice because of fear? Will anyone learn to protect the voiceless? This type of brokenness is perpetuated beyond the community once students graduate from the College, or faculty and staff transfer to other schools or employers. The poison of creating narratives like Hudson can become a way of life beyond College. This is a certain danger to our community and represents a failure of moral leadership.

The third element to be considered relates to the "absence of restorative justice." Can the Social Justice College be a Social Justice school without the conversation of restorative justice within its own walls? Is there an opportunity to "repair" the harm caused in the dispute? Restorative justice is perhaps a settlement of sorts. Meaning, one party seeks to restore a loss by not only restoring what was lost, but also by acknowledging wrong doing. An adjudicated settlement does not acknowledge wrongdoing although we suspect wrongdoing took place. Adjudicated settlements simply expel the notion of wrongdoing. Restorative justice involves acknowledgement of wrongdoing and a cooperative arrangement between effected parties to work toward fixing what was broken.

The fourth element is that of "reconciliation." It occurs when both parties actively seek to be a part of the healing process by virtue of an inward humility leading to an apology for one's actions and a demonstrable visible sign of a renewed healthy relationship devoid of manipulation in a world that is divided. One might think that a College founded upon religious principles embracing reconciliation would know how to participate in such an act – but the Hudson case is an excellent example of the inability of the College to know what it means to reconcile.

I believe victims remain victims for a lifetime. Without restorative justice and reconciliation, the wounds of the act of injustice remain unhealed in the face of wayward institutional power. Hudson will always be a victim. With this knowledge, I worry about students, faculty, and staff who are afraid to stand up against institutional power. If the College doesn't realize they lack the competence to be just, or understand the impact of denying a "voice in the room" to make a case for fairness, others may fall victim to injustice at the College as well. Another case like Hudson's could be the impetus of awakening others to injustice at the school, or, Hudson's case could be the blanket that smothers the honesty and courage to speak up and speak out against unfairness or threats of retaliation at the College. I fear it is the latter. The fear of retaliation can be real. It can act as a 'silencer' of voices who know the story. Hudson's case is instructive. Without a 'voice in the room,' her story was marginalized and invalidated as proven by the fact no one in the school of justice came to her defense. This of course, is the irony of the story. This is a book about 'justice' involving an institution that touts 'justice', which withheld justice from one of its own. It is a cautionary tale. Justice came with a hard price. Hudson's victory was hard won. Her emotional scars may take a long time to heal. She will always remember the threat of losing her financial security to care for her daughter. She will always remember the callousness of those who approved her termination, denied her appeal to return to work, and then supported the College's defense ending in a settlement.

I have learned from watching the actions of a College I love and support financially, that it is *easier to talk about justice, than to actually do justice*. The evidence in this book is my supporting testimony. I pray Philander Smith College will do the hard thing and do justice, so the College can mirror its mission to **"graduate academically accomplished students, grounded as advocates for social justice, determined to change the world for the better."**

It's easy to talk justice

There are books
that recite the stories of justice –
making it easy for others to talk about justice

There are people
who have fought for justice –
making it easy for others to talk about justice

There are laws
which define justice –
making it easy for others to talk about justice

Books may recite
People may have fought
Laws may define
It's easy to talk justice
But it is hard to achieve justice

—C.J. Duvall, Jr.

Notes

Introduction

Greg Schaffer, former co-worker commented on the duty to obey the law. "Right is right. If you witness a wrong, and do nothing, you might as well have done the wrong yourself." February 19, 2018.

Hudson versus Philander Smith College. Case 4:17-cv-00363-KGB. United States District Court Eastern District of Arkansas Western Division.

The four high ranking officials listed as defendants in the initial filing of Hudson versus Philander Smith College were: Kevin Cooper, Sericia Cole, Christopher Newton and Dr. Roderick Smothers.

Chapter One – One Against the Many

Wiesel, Elie. *"Hope, Despair and Memory."* Nobel Lecture. December 11, 1986.

"EEOC Releases Fiscal Year 2016 Enforcement and Litigation Data."
https://www.eeoc.gov/eeoc/newsroom/release/1-18-17a.cfm

"EEOC Implements Nationwide Procedures for Releasing Respondent Position Statements and Obtaining Responses from Charging Parties."
https://www.eeoc.gov/eeoc/newsroom/release/position_statement_procedures.cfm

Wiesel, Elie. Nobel Peace Prize Acceptance Speech. Oslo, Norway. December 10, 1986.
http://eliewieselfoundation.org/elie-wiesel/nobelprizespeech/

Observations on Hudson's performance versus the male directors based upon documented minutes and performance evaluation material during the period February 15, 2013 thru December 16, 2015.

Chapter Two – The Search for Truth

Philander Smith College. Position Statement. Charging Party: Gemessia Hudson, Charge No. 493-2016-00958. Respondent: Philander Smith College. May 2, 2016.

Stevenson, Bryan. Just Mercy. New York: Spiegel & Grau. 2014. Print.

Empower ME Tour with UNCF Las Vegas 2013! October 22, 2013.
http://meshelle.net/the-world-is-too-small-to-lie/

Gates Foundation Initiative Aims to Build Bridges to Student Achievement in Jacksonville, June 19, 2014.
http://news.wjct.org/post/gates-foundation-initiative-aims-build-bridges-student-achievement-jacksonville

RETWEET @dallasschools, December 9, 2014.
https://twitter.com/KDMalonson/status/542472101341712385

April 25, 2015 Scholarship Information Session in Little Rock, AR;
http://littlerock.eventful.com/events/uncf-scholarship-information-session-philande-/E0-001-083115074-8

September 18, 2015. Dillard University. Gates Millennium Scholars Program Presents Bridge Builders.
https://www.louisianabelieves.com/docs/default-

source/links-for-newsletters/new-orleans-recovery-district-updatedpdf.pdf?sfvrsn=2

November 15, 2015. UCLA. Gates Millennium Scholars' Program Presents Bridge Builders Program. https://www.ceed.ucla.edu/wp-content/uploads/ceed/Gates-Bridge-Builders-at-UCLA_Nov2015.pdf

UNCF Staff Announcements. "Please welcome Kevin Cooper." Copy held for subpoena of information. Notes include admissions counselor history and new hire as Relationship Manager for Outreach.

Chapter Three – Moral Leadership

Reist, L. Fitzgerald, et.al editors. *The Book of Discipline of the United Methodist Church*. Nashville, TN: The United Methodist Publishing House, 2016. Print.

Chapter Four – Retaliation

Martin Luther King – Acceptance Speech
https://www.nobelprize.org/prizes/peace/1964/king/26142-martin-luther-king-jr-acceptance-speech-1964/

"Retaliation – Making it Personal"
https://www.eeoc.gov/laws/types/retaliation_considerations.cfm

Chapter Five – Dialogue

Plato. Common attribution of the quote: "Your silence is consent."

Hudson versus Philander Smith College. Case 4:17-cv-00363-KGB. United States District Court Eastern District of Arkansas Western Division. June 1, 2017.

Uttinger, Dayton. *How much does it Cost to File a Civil Suit and When Should You?* Fiscal Tiger.com. January 19, 2018.

Chapter Six – Was It Worth It?

Winfrey, Oprah. "Cecil B. deMille Award Acceptance Speech." Golden Globes. 2018.

Hudson versus Philander Smith College. Case 4:17-cv-00363-KGB. United States District Court Eastern District of Arkansas Western Division. October 17, 2018.

Epilogue

Hudson versus Philander Smith College. Case 4:17-cv-00363-KGB. United States District Court Eastern District of Arkansas Western Division. April 30, 2018.

Acknowledgments

Although this book is brief, the development of this story required many hours of work and sacrifice over a three-year period. I give thanks to my wife Karen, and my daughters Alisha and Alana for tolerating my pre-dawn movement around the house, and late-night work hours. To complete this project, I received the immeasurable assistance of my Chief Editor, Erin Ray. Additional review and proof editing were provided by Victoria Mays, Garbo Hearne; as well as counsel from Jess Askew, J.D., Kutak Rock, LLP. There are many others deserving of acknowledgment whom either directly or indirectly contributed to my journey in the pursuit of justice. Thank you, Sister Tufara Waller Muhammad, Cultural Organizer and Strategist; Dr. Enoch Hammond Oglesby, my Christian Ethics professor at Eden Theological Seminary a son of Earle, Arkansas; Mr. Philip Grant Duvall, whose passion to fight for justice continuously spills into my path. I lift up the work of Dr. James Cone, an alum and former professor of Philander Smith College, author of *The Cross and the Lynching Tree*, a theological treatise which inspired me to investigate how Hudson was 'lynched' by her alma mater for speaking truth; and Dr. Lupita Rasheed, who quietly moved on to greater heights after being passed over for a promotion at Philander Smith College. I acknowledge the strength of Mr. Daryl Johnson in his path to recovery following the abandonment of friends, who could have been a "voice" but remained quiet in his hour of need. There are of course, my mentees, (now friends), who participated in acts of community service, aligning with my heart for a just world: Mr. Jeremy Tolbert, Ms. Alyshia Williams, Mr. David Wells, Ms. Francennett Herrera, Ms. Danielle Horton, Mr. Kirk Daniels, Mr. Paul Richards-Kuan, Mr. Dominque Fishback, Mr. Maurice Washington, Mr. Byron Johnson, Ms. Barbara Shipp, Ms. Paige Fisher, Mr. Joseph Bradley, Ms. Brittany James, Ms. Desirae Holmes, Mr. Ahmad Williams, Mr. Javonte Washington, Mr. Darryl Jackson (St. Louis), Ms. Tiarra Harris, Ms. Jasmine DeHart, Ms. Taylen Jackson, Ms. Meagan Patterson, Ms. Casey O'Hara, Ms. Anna Feldman, Mr. Josiah Jones, Mr. William Jones and Ms. Tiara Person. God speed to you all.

About the Author

C. J. Duvall, Jr., is a former Fortune 250 executive with more than 30 years of human resources background. Duvall holds a Bachelor's degree in Behavioral Science, a Master's degree in Industrial Organizational Psychology and a Master's of Theological Studies degree. Duvall served as a trustee, a visiting business school professor, a vice president of institutional advancement and a mentor to students of Philander Smith College. He received an honorary doctorate from Philander Smith and has a building on its campus named in his honor. He continues to support the school as a donor, encouraging them to act honestly and justly in their dealings with faculty, staff and students.

www.ingramcontent.com/pod-product-compliance
Lightning Source LLC
LaVergne TN
LVHW011845060526
838200LV00054B/4175